1

JACKSON'S VALLEY CAMPAIGN

By Capt. Douglas A. Cohn, U.S.A. (ret)

with maps from

THE WEST POINT ATLAS OF THE CIVIL WAR

From Aunt Connie Xmas 1993

1986
American Publishing Company
Washington, D.C.

ISBN 0-941625-00-1

For those who fought and for those who fell in Vietnam . . .

. . . and for America's Lost Causes

With Gratitude

My grandfather, G.L. Shaw, and my mother, Henrietta Cohn, for instilling the inspiration; my wife Kathryn, and our children, Colleen, Rachael, Elaine and Brian, for patient assistance; John Horan and the *Northern Virginia Daily* for promotion; Beverly Robin Trefny and Nora Sloyan for editing; Janet Nave and Henry Holt and Company for map reproductions; Susan Guynn for layout assistance; John Slonaker and the U.S. Army Military History Institute and Lola S. Wood and the Warren Rifles Confederate Museum for research assistance.

Introductory Notes and Definitions

All locations are in Virginia unless otherwise stated or made clear by context.

Strategy: war plans and maneuvers.
Operations: campaign plans and maneuvers (treated as strategy herein).
Tactics: battle plans and maneuvers.

C.S.A.: Confederate States of America or Confederate States Army.
U.S.V.: United States Volunteers

Guns: cannons.
Musket: smooth bore, individual firearm.
Rifle: rifled, individual firearm.

General: a full general, usually the commander of an army; also used to denote any general, including, in descending order: general, lieutenant general, major general, brigadier general. (First reference to an individual herein always indicates his full title).

Prior page: Maj. Gen. (later Lt. Gen.) Thomas Jonathan "Stonewall Jackson" in 1862. Courtesy Historic Lexington Foundation, Stonewall Jackson House.

CONTENTS

I. THE NATURE OF HIS GENIUS

"Jackson would have resorted to strategy if he had commanded a million men; he couldn't help it...He was the most rapid mover in the South."

— Col. Henry Kyd Douglas, Confederate States Army

It may well have been that Maj. Gen. (later Lt. Gen.) Thomas Jonathan Jackson, C.S.A., the general called "Stonewall," did not intend or plan all he accomplished. And it is argued that the perception of his genius and the brilliance of his Valley Campaign in the spring of 1862 are diminished as a result. Yet, this belies both the nature of his genius and the nature of war.

War is the realm of rapid change. Man's will and nature's weather change; heroes occasionally cower, and cowards occasionally steel themselves to circumstances; overestimations and underestimations, miscommunications and misunderstandings, mistakes and misplaced intentions all abound; friends are seemingly immobile and often unreliable, while foes are seemingly relentless and usually unpredictable; friends rarely perform as well — or foes as poorly — as a commander could reasonably expect; and even when most men perform their duties, most commanders fail because war has few winners. All this and more is the "fog of war."

Any commander who predicates plans upon precise calculations in such an endeavor is attempting to make science of art, and Napoleon said, "He who wishes to make quite sure of everything in war, and never ventures, will always be at a disadvantage. Boldness is the acme of wisdom." Stonewall Jackson made no such attempt, nor did he make any pretenses of perfection or of perfect foresight. He simply had a knack for choosing courses of action that were likely to compel his opponents to err. And he kept his profession in perspective: for him, as for the other great "captains of history," it was a profession devoid of certainty, but one in which mobility was superior to immobility, and action was superior to reaction.

Jackson explained his own military philosophy to a trusted subordinate, Capt. (later Brig. Gen.) John D. Imboden: "There are two things never to be lost sight of by a military commander: always mystify, mislead and surprise the enemy if possible; and when you strike and overcome him, never let up in your pursuit so long as your men have strength to follow; for an army routed, if hotly pursued, becomes panic-stricken and then can be destroyed by half their number. The other rule is never fight against heavy odds, if by any possible maneuvering you can hurl your own force on only part, and the weakest part, of your enemy and crush it. Such tactics will win every time, and a small army may thus destroy a large one in detail, and repeated victory will make it invincible."

Still, such thoughts were not new, and, ironically, part of Jackson's genius was his willingness to violate his own philosophy (see Chapter VII. The Battle of Kernstown). Only the phrase, "mystify, mislead and surprise," was really Jacksonian, because he was arguably the most secretive commander in history.

Later, in the midst of the Valley Campaign, he succinctly stated another tenet of his philosophy, this time to an irate lady from Winchester who had just scolded him for marching troops to the point of exhaustion. To her, he replied, "Legs are cheaper than heads, madam." He truly was "the most rapid mover in the South," and his infantry truly earned their unique sobriquet: "Jackson's Foot Cavalry."

Yet, for all his secrets and for all his speed, Stonewall Jackson's unstated, but foremost, military forte lay elsewhere: *diversion.* The Valley Campaign is still studied, not for the victories he attained, but for the defeats he averted. Jackson had the uncanny ability to divert his enemies from their primary objectives — and in 1862, the primary Federal objective in the East was Richmond and presumably the defending Army of Virginia (soon to be renamed the Army of Northern Virginia).

They did not do so in 1862, and Jackson was the reason. With never more than 17,000 men, Jackson enticed more than 60,000 Federals to or toward the Shenandoah Valley, where he played the fox to their hounds.

It could be said for each of Stonewall Jackson's actions, there was an *unequal* and opposite enemy reaction.

II. THE NATURE OF THE MAN

"...did it ever occur to you that General Jackson is crazy?"
—Maj. Gen. (later Lt. Gen.) Richard Ewell, C.S.A.

Bald, birdlike Gen. Richard Ewell, Jackson's highest ranking subordinate, had much to say, and most of it was colored with lisped expletives while his head tilted and his eyes bulged. But as odd as he was, Jackson was more so.

Stonewall Jackson was the archetypal eccentric genius, though initially, Ewell saw only the eccentricities and none of the genius. Yet, before the spring of '62 and the Valley Campaign were over, Ewell came to see only the genius and none of the eccentricities.

The correlation — if any — between idiosyncrasies and intellect was not applied to Gen. Jackson. Rather, these traits were viewed as separate phenomena in him. So people who ridiculed Jackson's behavior could praise his genius and literally follow him to the death.

When Gen. Ewell asked if Jackson was "crazy," he was addressing Col. (later Brig. Gen.) James A. Walker, who, as a student before the war, had challenged the then professor Jackson to a duel (which did not take place). "I don't know, General," Walker replied. "We used to call him 'Fool Tom' Jackson at the Virginia Military Institute, but I do not suppose he is really crazy."

A frustrated Ewell remained unconvinced: "I tell you he is as crazy as a March hare."

Ewell's frustration did not last long, and Walker went on to hold high rank and Jackson's high esteem. There is, however, no tale more poignant and more pertinent to the issue of Jackson's split reputation than that told of Brig. Gen. Richard Garnett. Garnett commanded Jackson's old unit (as Walker later would), the immortal Stonewall Brigade, but at the Battle of Kernstown, he ordered an unauthorized retreat when the brigade ran out of ammunition. For this, Jackson relieved him of command and preferred charges. Nothing came of this, but a pall hung over Garnett thereafter. (However, the lesson was learned, for later that year, at Second Manassas, Brig. Gen. Maxcy Gregg of Maj. Gen. A. P. Hill's division of Jackson's corps found himself in a similar position, and responded, "Tell General Hill that my ammunition is exhausted, but that I will hold my position with the bayonet.") Even so, when Jackson was killed in 1863, it was Garnett who said to the dead general's aides, "You know of the unfortunate breach between General Jackson and myself; I can never forget it, nor cease to regret it. But I wish to assure you that no one can lament his death more sincerely than I do. I believe he did me great injustice, but I believe also he acted from the purest motives. He is dead. Who can fill his place!" The aides then asked Gen. Garnett to serve as one of Gen. Jackson's pallbearers.

Only a few weeks later, at Gettysburg, Garnett fell victim to the lingering dichotomy of Jackson's idiosyncrasies and intellect. His reputation tarnished by the dead general he admired, Garnett sullenly, fatalistically, and with high visibility, led a brigade in Pickett's Charge. Every soldier in the Army of Northern Virginia knew Garnett would die to recoup his honor, and he fell on the field just yards from the Federal guns on Cemetery Ridge.

The man who wielded such influence, Thomas Jonathan Jackson, had given no early indications he would do so. Born in Clarksburg (now in West Virginia) in the western mountains of Virginia on 21 January 1824, he was orphaned and raised by relatives.

Due to one relative's connections, the young Jackson received an appointment to the United States Military Academy at West Point, New York, a position for which he was totally unprepared. There, the other cadets initially looked upon him as a poorly educated, seedy lout—an assessment that later proved to be as irrelevant as it was accurate.

Jackson's appearance was truly only superficial. He was 5 feet 10 inches tall, and his feet approached size 14. He was not, and never became, eloquent, charismatic, or impressive of bearing. Even Henry

Kyd Douglas, who greatly admired Jackson and served as a junior officer on his staff in 1862, would call him "the most awkward man in the army." By the Civil War, he had grown a dark, scraggly, rust-colored beard, but only the glow in the depth of his deep-set blue eyes was truly distinctive. So before he was called "Stonewall," he was called "Old Blue Light" because the light within him was not yet seen.

Cadet Jackson graduated 17th out of 59 in the Class of '46, a class filled with 24 future Civil War generals, including George B. McClellan (second in the class) and George Pickett (last in the class). McClellan, who would command the Federal Army of the Potomac in the spring of '62, and become the Democratic presidential nominee in '64, said Jackson would have passed him up if the course of study had gone on another year. Despite this, Jackson was not looked upon as brilliant, just industrious. With naive sincerity, Jackson furthered that image when he explained how he intended overcoming his academic shortcomings: "I can make it up in study."

Upon graduation, Jackson was commissioned a second lieutenant in the artillery and sent to war in Mexico, a war from which he emerged a brevet major with a distinguished record. However, he and the U.S. Army soon realized the peacetime army was not for him after he attempted to replace the sting of battle with petty quarrels and martial strictness. It all ended in 1852. The intransigent young officer resigned, moved to Lexington in the southern Shenandoah Valley and became a professor at Virginia Military Institute (VMI).

Jackson was married in 1853, widowed 14 months later, and remarried in 1857. Meanwhile, he developed hypochondria and discovered religion, both of which he embraced with his customary fervor (he had always been a mild hypochondriac, but after a severe post-Mexican War illness, the bouts of imagined maladies became more extreme).

He replaced military regimentation with a personal regimen consisting of near fanatical adherence to systematic scheduling, strict diet, prayers and punctuality. Even his devoted wife, Anna, the former Mary Anna Morrison, whom he considered "a gift from our Heavenly Father," lovingly said, "He never waited for anyone, not even his wife."

As to his diet and demeanor, Brig. Gen. (later Lt. Gen.) Richard Taylor (President Zachary Taylor's son) of Gen. Ewell's command wrote, "If silence be golden, he was a 'bonanza.' He sucked lemons, ate hard-tack, and drank water, and, I imagine, his idea of the 'whole duty of man' was—praying and fighting." And, "Where Jackson got his lemons 'no fellow could find out,' but he was rarely without one."

During the Valley Campaign, when Jackson's army was struggling to pass through the Federal trap at Strasburg, the men were pressed to keep the way open so a wagon train heavily laden with captured supples could get through. Taylor, ever the proponent of combat humor, wrote, "The men said his anxiety for the wagons was because of the lemons among the stores!"

Taylor, however, saw Jackson's other side and inner self:

"I dwelt on the rich harvest of glory he had reaped in his brilliant (Valley) campaign, and, observing him closely, caught a glimpse of the man's inner nature. It was but a glimpse. The curtain closed, and he was absorbed in prayer. Yet, in that moment, I saw an ambition, boundless as Cromwell's, and as merciless . . . . I have written that he was ambitious; and his ambition was vast, all-absorbing. . . he loathed it, perhaps feared it, but he could not escape it—it was himself; nor rend it—it was his own flesh. He fought it with prayer, constant and earnest—Appolyon and Christian in ceaseless combat. What limit to set to his ability I know not, for he was ever superior to occasion. Under ordinary circumstances it was difficult to estimate him because of his peculiarities—peculiarities that would have made a lesser man absurd . . ."

When Stonewall sat, he sat bolt upright, and when he studied, he stood. He claimed proper posture kept his organs in alignment and helped his legendary powers of concentration. In this manner he prepared the lessons for his VMI classes, but by all accounts, the seedy, sleepy-looking professor with a high-pitched drawl, who lectured by rote, was no academician. Unintentionally, the professor was actually preparing himself more than his unwilling students, because by teaching he was learning, and, among other subjects, he was teaching the history, strategy and tactics of military (particularly artillery) art. This was the primary career experience that set Jackson apart from almost all other military professionals who rose to high rank in the Civil War.

III. STONEWALL

"There stands Jackson like a stonewall."
—Brig. Gen. Barnard Bee

Thomas Jonathan Jackson learned his trade as a cadet at West Point, practiced it as an officer in the Mexican War and honed it as an instructor at VMI. It only remained for him to gain a modicum of experience at general-officer rank to complete his training. The rest would depend upon innate intellect and fate.

Fate was comprised of the Civil War and Jackson's association with VMI and the Shenandoah Valley. Shortly after the outbreak of war in the spring of 1861, Gen. Robert E. Lee, then commanding Virginia state forces, appointed Jackson commander of Virginia's troops in the Shenandoah. Also, Jackson was promoted to colonel, but that was not unusual for a West Pointer with Mexican War experience.

Shortly thereafter, when Virginia's forces were absorbed by the Confederate States of America, Brig. Gen. (later Gen.) Joseph E. Johnston was given the Valley command. Jackson was retained, however, promoted to brigadier general and given the brigade with which he would share immortality.

Jackson, Johnston and their men did not long remain in the Shenandoah. By mid-July 1861, one Federal army had moved into the Valley and another, larger one, under Brig. Gen. Irvin McDowell was marching south from Washington toward Brig. Gen. Beauregard's Confederate army at Manassas Junction. Beauregard was preparing to defend along Bull Run, but reinforcements were desperately needed, and Johnston answered the call — while young Col. J.E.B. Stuart and a small cavalry contingent screened his departure from the Valley.

Johnston's men were transported by train (though they did march about half the distance) to Manassas, where they bolstered Beauregard's lines. But before all of these reinforcements arrived, the Confederates were compelled to give way. It was then that Jackson's brigade of Valley men stood their ground in the midst of chaos and Brig. Gen. Bee spoke the immortal words: "There stands Jackson like a stone wall. Rally behind the Virginians." Moments later, Gen. Bee was mortally wounded, but Stonewall Jackson and the Stonewall Brigade had received their appellations, and the battle's tide was turned.*

In just over three months, obscure Professor Jackson had become Stonewall Jackson and a hero to the Confederacy. In the fall he would be promoted to major general and once again be given command of the small Confederate force defending the Shenandoah—replacing Gen. Johnston who would be appointed to command of all Confederate forces in Virginia.

All of the elements were now in place for Gen. Thomas Jonathan Jackson to join the ranks of history's great captains. The training was completed, and although the genius within him had yet to be revealed, it was primed and ready. And except for those unusual aspects of his makeup that enhanced concentration, the personality quirks would prove to be quite apart from his military genius.

*An uncorroborated source, one of Bee's staff officers, claimed the remark was intended to be derogatory—implying Jackson was standing rather than advancing. Neither the situation, the facts nor the participants give any credence to this claim.

IV. SHENANDOAH:
SHEATH OF THE CONFEDERACY

"I want you to make me a map . . ."
—Stonewall Jackson

Wedged west and east by mountains, sealed in the south by mountains, split by a mountain, Virginia's Shenandoah Valley tilts and opens only to the northeast.

The Shenandoah was a sheath, and an army drawn from it became a dagger pointing to Washington, Baltimore, Philadelphia and New York, but an army thrust into it pointed only to mountains: the Alleghenies, including the Shenandoah and Bull Pasture mountains, to the west; the Blue Ridge Mountains to the east; and massive Massanutten Mountain in between. These imposing geological edifices, these tree and stone obstacles, became Maj. Gen. Jackson's strategic allies—and apparently, his alone.

Other facts and features of the Valley also played a part. It was a breadbasket that supplied Confederate armies, a site of some industry and home to VMI, the "West Point of the South." Also, Richmond's shortest link with Chattanooga, the East Tennessee and Virginia Railroad, ran through the mountains south of the Valley. Such facts, however, tended to be amplified when observed out of strategic context. Even Stonewall Jackson wrote to his friend, Confederate Congressman Alexander Boteler, "If this Valley is lost, Virginia is lost." But Jackson was fallible, and in this instance, his judgment was flawed because much of the Valley spent much of the war in Federal hands, and neither Virginia nor the South fell as a result.

Further, there were many breadbaskets in the South, and Federals could and did threaten the railroad through more convenient passages than the Shenandoah Valley. (In 1863, the loss of that railroad proved to be noncritical when Confederate reinforcements for the Chickamauga Campaign were routed instead from Virginia to just south of Chattanooga via railroads in the Carolinas and Georgia.)

No, the Shenandoah's true military value lay in what it threatened rather than in what it protected or produced. Although the South was fighting a defensive war, it soon became apparent that the fighting would have to be carried into the North to force a favorable conclusion. Undoubtedly, fear of this threat was on Abraham Lincoln's mind when on 27 July 1861 he directed that three Southern sites must be seized: Memphis, Tennessee; Manassas Junction, Virginia; and—in the heart of the Shenandoah—Strasburg, Virginia. And this would not be the last time during the war that the Federal president would focus on Strasburg (see Chapter XI. Strasburg: Mr. Lincoln's Trap).

Lincoln did not select Strasburg for its beauty because the town was not then the pleasant place it is today, at least according to one Federal chaplain. He was with one of the units that occasionally occupied Strasburg, and he described it as the "dirtiest, nastiest, meanest, poorest, most shiftless town I have yet seen in all the shiftless, poor, mean, nasty dirty towns of this beautiful valley."

Strasburg, less than 60 miles due west of Washington, was considered critically important to Federal defenses. This little town at the northwestern foot of Massanutten Mountain was linked with Manassas Junction and Washington to the east by the Manassas Gap Railroad. Perpendicular to this, running on a north-south axis through the "nasty" little town was the Valley Turnpike, which would be dubbed the "long gray road" before the war was over. Macadamized all the way from Winchester south to Staunton, it was well-suited for soldiers known as "foot cavalry."

But the region's dominant feature created the map. Massanutten Mountain split the Valley, split the Shenandoah River and forever confused directions: the river's North Fork flows on the west side of the mountain; the South Fork flows on the east side; and the river flows south to north, so armies proceeding down the Valley were marching northward.

The North Fork bends eastward around Massanutten at Strasburg and flows about twelve miles to Front Royal where it joins the South Fork coming down the Luray Valley (that portion of the Shenandoah Valley between Massanutten and the Blue Ridge) and continues north to the Potomac River at Harper's Ferry.

So, as a result of roads, railroads and rivers, Front Royal was second only to Strasburg as an important Federal defensive point in the Valley. Massanutten and the forks of the Shenandoah had conspired to turn these two towns into military bottlenecks — providing the Federal armies were inclined to so use them.

Winchester, situated midway between Strasburg and Harper's Ferry, was the Valley's bustling city in 1862, and so it was prized and defended by both sides, even though it was not a naturally defensible place. During the war, several battles would be fought in and around the city, and it would trade hands 72 times. Stonewall Jackson established a headquarters there, and he and his men were well-loved by its citizens — a Federal cavalryman described it "as rebellious and aristocratic as it was beautiful." Despite this, Jackson was not one of the generals who attempted to defend it — although he twice attacked Federal armies that did. But then, the Federals were compelled to defend the B & O Railroad and the C & O Canal, the primary east-west transportation lines running through Harper's Ferry, and Winchester was the first sizeable, comfortable and convenient place for them to do so south of Harper's Ferry.

South, along the North Fork up the Valley from Strasburg, the towns of Woodstock and Mount Jackson would see some delaying actions, but the next town, New Market, was strategically important because the only pass through Massanutten Mountain lay just east of there.

Farther south, Harrisonburg and Conrad's Store (Elkton) anchored, respectively, the southwest and southeast termini of Massanutten. And just south of them and midway between, two obscure villages, Cross Keys and Port Republic, at the confluence of the South Fork tributaries, would eventually provide Jackson an opportunity to demonstrate the value of studying military history. There, he reenacted one of Napoleon's campaigns.

Finally, up the Valley Turnpike from Harrisonburg, the southern boundary of the Valley Campaign was marked by the town of Staunton and the east-west running tracks of the Virginia Central Railroad.

Overall, the Valley was an operational area that provided many opportunities and much confusion. Accurate measurements, whether of distance or altitude, were not commonplace there in 1862, and yet accurate maps were essential to those who would lead others in war. Even so, in 1862, only one general in the Shenandoah Valley seemed to fully appreciate the value of cartography.

Following the Battle of Kernstown, Stonewall Jackson added cartographer Jedediah Hotchkiss to his staff and told him, "I want you to make me a map of the Valley, from Harper's Ferry to Lexington, showing all the points of offense and defense." Hotchkiss, a transplanted New Yorker and a teacher by trade, had founded two schools in the Valley, but map making was his passion, and one which he had already put to use for Robert E. Lee in 1861.

Like many another individual before and since, Hotchkiss was captivated by the Shenandoah. The Valley is one of those fertile, scenic sites where man and nature meld as if they had always been intended to do so. From the arsenal at Harper's Ferry to VMI at Lexington, the people of the Shenandoah Valley blend a patriotic, martial air with gentle Southern politeness, and the whole Valley emanates history. These are root-creating qualities, and the Valley, its river and its people have always employed them to captivate and capture.

V. THE CHAINS OF COMMAND

"I do not forget that I was satisfied with your arrangement to leave [Gen.] Banks at Manassas, but when that arrangement was broken up and nothing was substituted for it, of course I was not satisfied. I was constrained to substitute something for it myself."
—Abraham Lincoln to Maj. Gen. McClellan

Only one United States President, Abraham Lincoln, ever took Article II, Section 2 of the U.S. Constitution literally and exercised his power as "Commander in Chief of the Army and Navy" (President Washington led troops during the Whiskey Rebellion, but before the army saw what limited action there was, he relinquished command to Gen. "Light-Horse Harry" Lee, father of Gen. Robert E. Lee).

The Civil War began with brevet Lt. Gen. Winfield Scott, "Old Fuss and Feathers" of Mexican War (and the War of 1812) fame, in command of all Federal armies, but Maj. Gen. George B. McClellan, "Little Mac," soon conspired and contrived to replace him. In November 1861, he succeeded, but it was an unsavored success because Lincoln became impatient with McClellan's procrastinating and assumed the general-in-chief duties himself 11 March 1862.

McClellan was allowed to retain command of the principal Federal army in the east, the Army of the Potomac, which he had been planning to lead into Virginia for some time. His plan called for transporting the army by ship from Washington to Fort Monroe near Norfolk. From there, he would march it overland, up the Peninsula between the York and James rivers and threaten Richmond—theoretically, Gen. Johnston's defending Confederate army would be destroyed in the process. (Originally, McClellan had planned to land at Urbana on the Rappahannock River, but that idea was abandoned when the Confederate army marched south from Manassas to Culpeper.)

In any event, Lincoln used the Peninsula operations to justify his command shuffling. He reasoned that McClellan would not be in a position to communicate in a timely manner with the other Federal armies from the Peninsula. So, despite the fact that experience and tradition had altered the Constitutional clause to mean civilian "control" rather than civilian "command" of the military, Lincoln took command.

Except in the Eastern Theater of War (Maryland, Virginia and the region that would become West Virginia), however, distance and geography confined Lincoln's military influence to general directives. In 1862, that exception seemed perfectly suited for commanding from Washington. Relatively new inventions, the telegraph and railroad, appeared to offer the means (the Federal government was authorized by Congress on 31 January 1862 to take over both of these when the public safety was threatened). There could be no denying that messages could be quickly communicated — providing the telegraph lines remained intact — or that messengers and troops could be rapidly transported — providing they were transported to points on or near rail lines and providing those lines remained open But the technology was overrated, and the demands for constant, accurate and understandable communications could not be met so far from the fronts.

Then there was the problem of the commander. Lincoln, except for some insignificant junior-officer service during the Black Hawk War, was devoid of military experience, training and study, and he delighted in recounting his inept martial experiences. Even so, after McClellan's departure for the Peninsula, Lincoln did not retain a competent military advisor. Instead, he and Secretary of War Stanton began reading books on strategy. These facts were well known by the various Federal field commanders, so they endeavored to use distance as an insulating ally.

While retaining general control over all of the Federal armies, Lincoln asserted specific, day-to-day direction over the forces near

Washington, the defense of which he seemed to regard as his personal responsibility. So while broad directives were issued to McClellan and the other major field commanders, the three separate Federal armies in the Washington area received his very specific daily, and sometimes hourly, instructions.

These various armies were designated as "departments," and in the spring of '62, the three most directly controlled by Lincoln were: the Mountain Department (located just west of the Shenandoah Mountains in what would become West Virginia), created 11 March 1862, commanded by Maj. Gen. William Rosecrans until 29 March and by Maj. Gen. John C. Fremont thereafter; the Department of the Rappahannock (at Fredericksburg), created 4 April 1862, commanded by Maj. Gen. Irvin McDowell; and the Department of the Shenandoah, also created 4 April 1862, commanded by Maj. Gen. Nathaniel P.Banks.

As the Valley Campaign got into full swing, the Federal chain of command was actually quite unified and logical — that is the chain was logical, but the command was flawed. The opposite situation prevailed in the Confederacy.

Politically moderate Confederate President Jefferson Davis, West Point Class of 1828, was considered the appropriate choice to lead the Southern Nation in war. He had served in the Mexican War and later become U.S. Secretary of War, but despite such credentials, he did not overrate his own military prowess, and he aggressively sought, and often obtained — with some disastrous exceptions — high military talent. (Of note is the fact that Davis of Mississippi and Lincoln of Illinois were both born in Kentucky, less than 100 miles and one year apart from each other).

Virginians Robert E. Lee and Joseph E. Johnston graduated from West Point in 1829, and they too fought in the Mexican War, and both of them remained in the army until their state seceded. In 1861, Johnston performed admirably at First Manassas, but the same could not be said of Lee's operations in western Virginia. So the following year, Johnston was the commander of Confederate forces in Virginia, and Lee was the chief military advisor to Jefferson Davis.

Johnston's position was defined; Lee's was not. His was a position of responsibility without authority. Between Johnston and Davis, however, a personal schism existed that apparently dated back to their cadet days.

This command system worked until distance intervened. When Johnston and his army marched from Manassas to Culpeper to southeast of Richmond in response to McClellan's efforts on the Peninsula, his outlying forces in Fredericksburg, the Shenandoah Valley and southwestern Virginia became more difficult to coordinate and control, and Gen. Lee stepped into the void.

The force most affected by this loose structure was Stonewall Jackson's Valley Army, for unlike the Federal armies under Lincoln, the Confederate structure in Virginia was wholly lacking in unity of command. Lee, being in the Confederate capital and communications center of Richmond, was closer to Jackson than Johnston was, and he spoke for the president. Therefore, the situation evolved with Johnston issuing infrequent orders and Lee sending continuous suggestions.

Since Jackson was never detached from Johnston's command, Lee's messages should have created serious conflicts and problems. This loose system, instead, benefited Jackson. Because he received what amounted to two sets of often conflicting orders, Jackson was occasionally able to choose the instructions of his choice or even to mix them until they coincided with his own concepts. He was essentially left free to conduct his campaign, and leave Lee and Johnston to iron out their differences like the classmates, friends and gentlemen he knew them to be.

So, in 1862, the Shenandoah Valley belonged to Stonewall Jackson. Brig. Gen. Edward Johnson commanded a very small force (3,000 men) called the Army of the Northwest that was opposing Federal moves in the mountains west of Staunton, and Maj. Gen. Richard Ewell commanded the division Johnston had left behind to "possibly" assist Jackson. Yet, both Johnson and Ewell continued to receive orders from Johnston and Lee, facts which slightly delayed, but otherwise interfered not at all with Jackson's plans. He simply absorbed both commands into the Valley Army (see Chapters VIII and IX).

Stonewall Jackson projected the image of obedience, but once the campaign began, Jackson the obedient became Jackson the autonomous. It truly was Jackson's Valley Campaign.

VI. ORDERS

"I wish the Yankees were in Hell!"
"I don't. Old Jack would follow
them there, with our brigade in front!"
— Two Southern soldiers

Stonewall Jackson expected to be obeyed as he himself obeyed — or so it seemed. He was strict, exacting and absolute, and yet truth belied impression. His fertile, creative mind was innovative, imaginative and, as events would prove, quite inclined to interpret rather than unquestionably accept orders. So, contrary to the popular image, he who would command was not easily commanded.

Jackson was at his best with independent commands — as in the Shenandoah — or with broad discretionary orders — as at the Second Battle of Manassas (Bull Run) later in '62 and, to some extent, the Battle of Chancellorsville in '63. Conversely, he did not do at all well when he received specific and restrictive orders as in the Seven Days' Battles that directly followed his Valley Campaign. Gen. Robert E. Lee, under whom he served during the Seven Days, never again made the same mistake with Jackson. Instead, he thereafter gave his great subordinate the maximum amount of latitude — a modus operandi that would, when applied to others (see Addendum A., "Ewell"), cost Lee terribly after Jackson's death. It was a fact Lee acknowledged when he said of his defeat at Gettysburg, "Jackson was not there."

In the Shenandoah in '62, it was to this independent subordinate, Stonewall Jackson, that Gen. Johnston issued operative orders for the coming campaign.

Johnston, facing McClellan's apparently overwhelming 155,000 man Army of the Potomac, was preparing to move his 40,000

Confederates south from Manassas to Culpeper. From there he could counter either a Federal overland thrust or an amphibious landing east of Fredericksburg. Clearly, Gen. Jackson's virtually insignificant 3,600 man Valley Army was little more than a covering force for Johnston's left flank, and this was reflected in Johnston's 1 March orders to him: retreat in concert with the main Confederate army so as to protect the strategic flank, secure the Blue Ridge passes and prevent Gen. Banks' 23,000 Federals from leaving the Valley.

The last of these was a tall order for 3,600 soldiers, but only if Banks began an eastward movement, which he was not likely to do as long as McClellan operated between Washington and Johnston's army. On 17 March 1862 everything changed.

Gen. McClellan's planned turning movement against Johnston by means of an amphibious landing had been reluctantly approved by Lincoln, but only with several provisos. Before McClellan could begin, the B & O Railroad and the C & O Canal must be made secure. McClellan agreed, and, accordingly ordered Gen. Banks to move south up the Shenandoah and establish a defensive posture at Winchester, following which he was to march the bulk of his command to Manassas. This part of Banks' mission emanated from Lincoln's other provisos as contained in his written orders (routed through Secretary of War Stanton) to McClellan:

"The President, having considered the plan of operations agreed upon by yourself and the commanders of army corps, makes no objection to the same, but gives the following direction as to its execution: 1st. Leave such force at Manassas Junction as shall make it entirely certain that the enemy shall not repossess himself of that position and line of communication. 2nd. Leave Washington entirely secure."

Lincoln was clearly asserting the role of General-in-Chief of the Army he had so recently taken from McClellan. And Lincoln's reference to the "commanders of the army corps," showed a further erosion of confidence in McClellan, the implication being that Lincoln was looking to a council of corps commanders to oversee McClellan.

On 17 March 1862, 400 ships began transporting the bulk of McClellan's army, minus McClellan who initially remained behind at his Alexandria headquarters, to Fort Monroe. However, because Gen. McDowell's I Corps of 30,000 men was *temporarily* left behind at Manassas, McClellan's orders to Banks — whose command was still in the Army of the Potomac — were altered. Instead of immediately transferring most of his force east of the Valley, he was instructed to proceed south from Winchester and drive Jackson from the Shenandoah.

This was the situation as 17 March dawned: Banks', like McClellan, was moving south. Jackson's tiny army was falling back before him, but his cavalry under Col. Turner Ashby maintained an active screen — much as J.E.B. Stuart had done a year earlier in the First Manassas (Bull Run) Campaign against Banks' predecessor.

The Federal cavalry, unable to penetrate Ashby's screen, drew the illogical and unsupported conclusion that Jackson's infantry had left the Valley, and this triggered the second part of Banks' mission. On 20 March, Gen. Shields' division was pulled back north to Winchester, and Gen. Williams' division was dispatched for Manassas. Banks himself was with Gen. Sedgwick's division at Harper's Ferry.

The "impossible," offensive part of Jackson's mission had therefore become operative. Banks must be held to the Valley.

VII. THE BATTLE OF KERNSTOWN

"It was reported that they were retreating, but I guess they are retreating after us."
— A Confederate cavalryman

"I think I may say I am satisfied, sir."
— Maj. Gen. Jackson

Stonewall Jackson won the only battle he ever lost. This military contradiction occurred just south of Winchester at a village called Kernstown.

With the departure of much of McClellan's Army of the Potomac for the Peninsula and Banks' dispatching of men out of the Valley, the Federal southeasterly rotation had begun. And it was as inexorable as it was strategically correct—from a Federal point of view. If it continued, Johnston's army would be overwhelmed and Richmond would be captured. How could Gen. Jackson and 3,600 Confederate soldiers possibly hope to prevent it?

Still, Jackson confidently wrote:

"Strasburg, *March* 23, 1862 — 6.50 a.m.
General Joseph E. Johnston,
Commanding Department of Northern Virginia:
MY DEAR GENERAL: With the blessing of an ever-kind Providence I hope to be in the vicinity of Winchester this evening..."

Stonewall Jackson was going after Nathaniel "Napoleon" P. Banks.

What precipitated this was Col. Ashby's report that all of Banks' Federals had left Strasburg, and all but four Federal regiments (approximately 3,200 men) had left Winchester and the Valley for Manassas. Shields' maneuvering instilled this idea in the minds of several Winchester citizens who then duly reported to Ashby.

In response, as Jackson's letter indicated, the Valley Army was rushing northward in pursuit. Indeed, it was obligated to do so if Banks' departure was to be prevented. So north, down the Valley Turnpike they marched, and their stragglers strewed the roadsides. On the late afternoon of the 23rd, the lead elements approached Kernstown and found Ashby's troopers hotly engaged with an enemy of undetermined strength.

It was Sunday, the day's sunlight and Jackson's men were nearly exhausted, and Jackson did not have time to conduct his own reconnaissance—all reasons why Jackson preferred to wait until the following day to fight. But it was not to be. Ashby's men had already been pushed back from some high ground, and this afforded the Federals a view of much of the Valley Army's dispositions.

The Southerners would have to make do. Straggling had reduced the Valley Army to 3,087 infantrymen, 290 cavalrymen and 27 pieces of artillery, numbers Jackson deemed sufficient. In any event, the battle was already joined.

A quick survey convinced Jackson that the Federals at Kernstown were strong and well-prepared. Consequently, Ashby, with the aid of Col. Burks' small brigade, was ordered to feint there while Jackson maneuvered his other two brigades a mile westward in a flanking movement toward the high ground of Sandy Ridge. Col. Fulkerson's brigade was on the left, and Jackson's old Stonewall Brigade, now under Brig. Gen. Garnett, was on the right, but the Federals were waiting as the Confederates went in.

Federal troops began pouring out of woods in front of the Southerners. Charges and countercharges occurred in rapid succession. Yet, still more Federal flags at the head of still more Federal troops kept materializing. Something was wrong.

On top of the ridge a stone wall ran between the lines, and both sides rushed for its safety. Fulkerson's men won the race, and their deadly fire from cover stopped the oncoming Northerners, only to face wave upon wave of additional Federal formations. Something was very wrong.

Belatedly, Jackson sent young Sandie Pendleton of his staff to reconnoiter from a high knoll. The suspected and unwelcome report was quickly returned: the Valley Army was facing at least 10,000 Federal troops! Jackson could only respond, "Say nothing about it; we are in for it."

If he could only hold on until nightfall, all might yet come well. He could extricate his army and know he had bloodied Banks and probably forced him to remain in the Valley. But it was not Jackson's day, and once again his plans were not to be. Since the battle commenced, Jackson had been giving conflicting orders, especially to Garnett, and he had also issued instructions to regimental commanders without informing their brigade commanders he was doing so. And instead of being near the firing line, he was well back, prodding fresh units forward. So when Garnett's men ran out of ammunition, Garnett was faced with the critical dilemma of the day. If the Stonewall Brigade was pulled out, Fulkerson's right flank would be left uncovered; if the Stonewall Brigade remained, it would be swamped by superior numbers. Jackson was not available, time was critical and Garnett, alone with the problem, decided. He pulled his men out, and of necessity, Fulkerson followed suit.

Jackson was just coming up with the reserve regiment when he was confronted with his army's retreat. "Go back and give them the bayonet," he commanded, but to no avail as the retreat was becoming a rout.

The reserves delayed a Federal pursuit, and finally, mercifully, darkness descended.

THE COST

Confederate: 80 killed, 375 wounded, 263 missing — total 718.
Federal: 118 killed, 450 wounded, 22 missing — total 590.

Tactically, Kernstown was a disaster for Jackson. His brilliance was missing; his presence was missed. Having been a successful brigade commander himself, Jackson assumed competence in his brigade commanders, and it was an assumption that naturally led to unsupervised delegation of authority. In fact, his subordinates were generally quite competent. It was just that they were not Stonewall Jackson.

In the future he would have to do more than direct the campaign and plan the battles; he would have to supervise them as well. Even so, one more battle would be required to convince him of the point.

Strategically, Kernstown was another matter. Brig. Gen. James Shields, whose Federal division fought the battle, reported on the 23rd: "The enemy's strength was about 15,000." And although he reduced the figure to "absolutely 11,000" two days later, Jackson's army was deemed to be large and capable of becoming larger if reinforced by Brig. Gen. Edward Johnson's men in the southern part of the Valley or by detachments from Johnston's army, then at Culpeper or by militia units from all over the Valley. It never occurred to Shields or to his superior, Banks, or to any other Federal commander that Jackson had simply attacked in error, believing the Federal force to be small.

But then, it was a time of exaggeration. McClellan was claiming Johnston's 40,000 man army actually exceeded 100,000, and this only served to make Shields' figures not only plausible, but probable — this even though Shields was not at the Battle of Kernstown. (He had been wounded in a skirmish the previous day, so Col. Nathan Kimball had actually commanded on the field, and it was Kimball who had refused to be taken in by Ashby's feint and moved his brigade to help thwart Jackson's flanking movement).

The result of all this was that Jackson had achieved the impossible. The southeasterly rotation of Federal troops was temporarily stopped and partially reversed. Lincoln refused to allow McDowell's corps (30,000 men) to leave for the Peninsula; Williams' division (7,000 men) was ordered back to Banks in the Valley; Blenker's division (7,000 men) was sent to reinforce Fremont (who had replaced Rosecrans) in the mountains west of the Valley; and, of course, Shields division of Banks' corps (9,000 men) was instructed to stay in the Valley. Then on 4 April, Lincoln removed the forces of Banks and McDowell from McClellan's command altogether.

Meanwhile, Johnston's Confederates were moving to the southeast, away from Jackson, to counter McClellan on the Peninsula. He did leave Gen. Ewell's division behind, but east of the Blue Ridge, to "cooperate" with Jackson, and he left a small 2,000-man brigade at Fredericksburg to "watch" McDowell.

So in the two weeks following Kernstown, the situation had changed dramatically. Fremont (including Blenker's division) and Banks now each had 15,000 men, McDowell was not far away with another 30,000, and this did not include the Washington garrison or the militia units in Maryland and Pennsylvania. Although Lincoln had always demanded that a sizable force be left to cover Washington, and Jackson had unintentionally attacked a much larger force than intended, these new Federal deployments were caused by Stonewall. Had he reconnoitered or been armed with proper information, the Battle of Kernstown would still have been fought—though undoubtedly after Federal strength had been significantly lowered due to departures for Manassas. In any event, tactical success was not the important element at Kernstown.

Jackson's final lines of his full, formal battle report placed the situation in perspective:

"Though Winchester was not recovered, yet the more important object for the present, that of calling back troops that were leaving the valley, and thus preventing a junction of Banks' command with other forces, was accomplished, in addition to his heavy loss in killed and wounded. Under these circumstances I feel justified in saying, that though the field is in possession of the enemy, yet the most essential fruits of the battle are ours."

So Jackson had good reason to say, "I am satisfied, sir." He had lost tactically, but far more importantly, won strategically, thereby winning the only battle he ever lost.

VIII. MASTER STROKE:
THE BATTLE OF McDOWELL

"You must use your judgment and discretion in these matters..."
— R.E. Lee, *General*

"I am leaving for the west in great haste."
— Stonewall Jackson

Gen. Banks wrote Secretary Stanton from Harrisonburg 28 April, "Our force is entirely secure here. The enemy is in no condition for offensive movements..." Later that day he continued, "If Jackson retreats from his present position (at Swift Run Gap) there is no reason for our remaining longer in this valley. If he does not, we can compel his retreat or destroy him. Then a small force, two or three regiments, falling back to Strasburg, which has been fortified for this purpose, will safely hold all that is important to the Government in this valley."

Two days later he reported that Jackson's command had departed for Richmond and that "there is nothing more to be done by us in this valley."

Then, totally oblivious to the dangerous reality of Jackson, Banks lamented to Stanton on 3 May, "I shall grieve not to be included in the active operations of this summer." But if Lincoln and Stanton did not plan to include him, he need not have grieved, for Jackson would soon include him to the point of legitimate grief.

Gen. Shields had, on 20 April, already bypassed Banks and written directly to Stanton, "There are no troops needed at present in the Shenandoah Valley but those which are necessary to garrison the different posts."

Lincoln complied. The pursuit after Kernstown had apparently rendered Jackson ineffective, and, in any event, the Valley was secondary to Lincoln's plans. Further, McClellan, now on the Peninsula, was pleading for McDowell's newly constituted army to support him by moving against Richmond from the north. The grand scheme, the march on Richmond, was the play, and Jackson was an unwanted distraction. On 1 May, Banks was ordered to withdraw to Strasburg, and the following day Shields was ordered to take his leave of Banks and march his division — which constituted half of Banks' army — out of the Valley to join McDowell at Fredericksburg. But these men were not "rapid movers," and it was not until 12 May that Banks and Shields started for their respective destinations.

Reality was otherwise. Following the Battle of Kernstown, Jackson had added to his small army by attracting fresh recruits from the Valley, which brought his strength up to about 6,000 men. Also, Brig. Gen. Edward Johnson's 3,000 man division, the remnant of the Confederate Army of the Northwest, which was situated in the mountains west of Staunton, was placed under Jackson's command, and Maj. Gen. Ewell's 8,000 man division was waiting east of the Blue Ridge to "cooperate." Additionally, Jackson could draw on the VMI cadets at Lexington. With potentially 17,000 men, Jackson's army was at the apex of its strength.

Jackson's 6,000 men were then in and around Conrad's Store (Elkton) and Swift Run Gap, in a classic flanking position. If Banks proceeded south, Jackson could strike at his supply lines. If Banks struck directly for Jackson, the Southerners could easily defend themselves in the mountains, and Ewell could come to their assistance. It was an interesting game. Instead of confronting Banks, Jackson was offering him the Valley, virtually daring him to take it, but Federal logic seemed to dictate that the dare be refused. Neither Lincoln nor Banks guessed that by refusing to do what Jackson apparently wanted them to do, they were in fact doing precisely what he wanted. So Banks went as far south as Harrisonburg, but no farther, even though the Confederate supply point and rail hub of Staunton was wide open and the key to linking forces with Fremont.

Meanwhile, Maj. Gen. Fremont's 8,000 Federals were strung out from the Potomac south to the hamlet of McDowell, and Brig. Gen. Blenker's 7,000 troops were enroute to join him. Fremont's lead elements were clearly moving on Staunton. Only Johnson's 3,000 Confederates stood in the way, and they were retreating.

By 3 May the Federals' secondary theater of war in the East, the Shenandoah Valley Campaign, had turned into a marching exercise with comic opera overtones: While Fremont's advance elements were pressing eastward through the Shenandoah Mountains toward Staunton, Blenker's division was passing westward through Winchester to join the tail of Fremont's column; Banks' army, which was then spread between Harrisonburg and New Market, was under orders to pull away from Staunton, north to Strasburg and thereupon detach Shields' division which was to move eastward to join McDowell at Fredericksburg. This meant that Shields and Blenker would, within days of each other, practically cross paths as they marched in diametrically opposite directions. This amateurish handling emanated from Washington despite sound advice to the contrary from both McDowell and Rosecrans (who was still in the Valley to expedite Blenker's movement).

McDowell wanted both Blenker's and Shields' divisions for his army — the implication being that both Fremont and Banks ought to go on the defensive. On the other hand, Rosecrans thought Blenker should be sent to Banks instead of Fremont. He reasoned that such a transfer would allow Banks to busy Jackson while Fremont took Staunton. Lincoln disagreed, and the orders stood. So while Banks was going over to the defensive, Fremont alone was continuing the Federal offensive in the area. There had to be a Southern opportunity in all this.

Throughout April, Jackson had been itching to get at his enemies, but Johnston's orders had specified a defensive role for him. Gen. Lee, on the other hand, was pressing for plans and actions, and on 29 April, Jackson, still at Swift Run Gap, offered some options and opinions and virtually charted the course of the Valley Campaign:

"As I do not believe that Banks will advance on me in my present position, I am disposed... to adopt one of three plans, viz, either to leave General Ewell here to threaten Banks' rear in the event of his advancing on Staunton, and move with my command rapidly on the force in front of General Edward Johnson, or else, cooperating with General Ewell, to attack the enemy's detached force between New Market and the Shenandoah, and, if successful in this, then to press forward and get in Banks' rear at New Market, and thus induce him to fall back; the third is to pass down the Shenandoah to Sperryville, and thus threaten Winchester via Front Royal.... Of the three plans I give the preference to attacking the force west of Staunton, for, if successful, I would afterward only have Banks to contend with, and in doing this would be reinforced by General Edward Johnson...."

At this time, Gen. Ewell was also writing to Gen. Lee, urging that a unified Confederate command be implemented. He also implied that his division could be better utilized in the Fredericksburg area. Ewell was not then subordinate to Jackson, and both men were still part of Johnston's command, yet both men were reporting to and receiving orders from Lee. But, of course, at the time, Johnston had his hands full at Yorktown on the Peninsula.

In any event, Robert E. Lee was perhaps the only man in the Confederate command to comprehend and appreciate what Jackson was about to do. He ordered Ewell to stand by to either support Jackson or to move on Fredericksburg. And he wrote Jackson his concurrence with the plan to attack Fremont, but he added that the decision was being left to Jackson's "judgment and discretion."

The logic of Jackson's plan seemed apparent — if studied in a vacuum. But the calmly worded dispatches of Jackson and Lee were contemplated and considered in the midst of strategic turmoil, and Jackson's plan was truly born of courage as much as brilliance. On 3 May, McClellan broke through the Confederate defenses at Yorktown, and Johnston's army began its retreat toward Richmond; at Fredericksburg, only a very small Confederate force stood between McDowell's 30,000 Federals and Richmond; and if Jackson split the Southern forces in the Valley, leaving Ewell at Swift Run Gap while he himself went off into the mountains, would not the Federals have an opportunity to strike a fatal blow in the Shenandoah as well — hitting Jackson and Ewell separately and thereby defeat them in detail? Was not Jackson playing into Federal hands by being drawn into the mountains, ever farther from Richmond? And even if he defeated part of Fremont's force, what benefit would come of it? Further, to get at Fremont, he would have to come out of the Blue Ridge and cross in the open past Banks.

Still, Jackson's small force was the only maneuverable Southern army left in Virginia. If he failed, Johnston would fail and Richmond would fall. The "ifs" were many, the resources were few, the chain of command was convoluted and yet intrepid intellect still made the decisions seem measured and rational. It was then, between 29 April and 3 May, that Jackson proposed and Lee approved the plans for the campaign: Jackson would unite with Edward Johnson, strike Fremont, return to the Valley, unite with Ewell and strike Banks, after which he would either move against McDowell at Fredericksburg or join in the fight against McClellan before Richmond. Speed was everything, and who better to carry it out than the "most rapid mover in the South?"

About this time a unity of mind and spirit was congealing between Jackson and Lee to such an extent that trust began replacing orders. There was between these dissimilar men of like minds an invisible bond that transcended the bounds of space and speech. And after Jackson was killed in '63, Lee would say, "I had such implicit confidence in Jackson's skill and energy that I never troubled myself to give him detailed instructions. The most general suggestions were all that he needed."

Such mental unity made Jackson's master stroke more comprehensible. Without waiting for Lee's approval, but never doubting it would come, he called Ewell's division up into Swift Run Gap and initiated his preferred plan. Ewell's men passed through Jackson's camp late on 29 April, but by the following morning, Jackson's troops were gone. Stonewall had marched south to Port

Republic, then, to virtually everyone's surprise, east over Brown's Gap and out of the Valley. That was on 3 May. The Valley men were going to Richmond after all to join Johnston's hard pressed army.

They arrived at Meachum's River Station to board trains the next day, but the engines were facing the wrong way. They were facing west. Surely the army had not trod through deep valley mud and over a high mountain pass only to take a train to whence they had come. But if there were lingering doubts about destinations, the first tug of the train reoriented the sceptics. They were indeed going back to the Valley. They arrived at Staunton later that day.

The mud march from Swift Run Gap to Port Republic to Meachum's accomplished three things. First, it reinforced the Federal belief that Jackson's army, a beaten force, was leaving the Valley. Second, such a route precluded a confrontation with Banks in the open which the direct route between Port Republic and Staunton would quite likely have forced. Third, he was able to use the railroad to achieve speed and surprise.

Here was Jackson's genius at its best. As the Confederates marched south to Port Republic, Banks sent word to Fremont that Jackson might be headed his way through Staunton. On 4 May, Fremont duly passed this information on to Brig. Gen. Milroy who commanded his lead brigade in the mountains east of the hamlet of McDowell.

Milroy replied on the 6th with sceptical certainty, "He (Jackson) cannot move from Port Republic toward my advanced position without leaving Banks in his rear..." Jackson's move was obviously a feint.

By then, Banks was wiring Stanton that "Ewell's division seems intended to replace Jackson's force which is greatly demoralized and broken." In other words, Ewell now occupied the flanking position, and Jackson was no longer a viable threat to Fremont or any other Federal force. Jackson's march out of the Valley had achieved its purpose.

So here was Milroy, certain Banks would prevent an attack by

Jackson, while Banks was equally certain that Jackson was gone and that Ewell was the only threat. Accordingly, Banks withdrew from Harrisonburg to New Market. All the while, Jackson was already in Staunton. Having arrived on the 4th, he sealed off the city and received the VMI cadets as temporary reinforcements. Then, on the 7th, he wrote Ewell, "I am leaving for the west in great haste."

Meanwhile, Milroy continued pressing eastward, ever closer to Jackson's trap while Banks pulled ever farther northward. As at Swift Run Gap, Jackson was employing two tiers of logic. He had feinted toward an obvious objective over a clearly perilous route, and, as intended, fooled no one. Then, he reinforced his opponents' preconceptions by withdrawing from the Valley, leaving Ewell's division in his old position. This seemed to be nothing more than one division relieving another, and because it was a fresh division of uncertain size, it was considered a threat.

So who would question Jackson's purpose in marching for the rail line at Meachum's? Why would he march so far east except to embark for Richmond? Yet, by abandoning the Valley and leaving Edward Johnson to his apparent fate, Jackson accomplished all he desired. The Valley Campaign would bear no finer example of his brilliance and bravery.

Impending disaster came with the dawn on the 7th for Milroy's Federals. Scouts came in with the first startling news of Jackson's presence on this isolated secondary front of this secondary theater of war. Milroy immediately ordered a retreat and sent urgent messages for help, signing one, "In haste." His 3,500 men were then in the mountains east of McDowell. Edward Johnson's Confederates were beginning to press them, and Jackson's men were close at hand.

Brig. Gen. Robert Schenck, at Franklin to the northwest, was the nearest Federal help, and as such was the recipient of Milroy's pleas. He dutifully passed the information along to Gen. Fremont, while he started his brigade marching hard for McDowell.

Milroy attempted to delay his pursuers in the mountains, but with

Johnson hard on his heels and Jackson always seeking to flank him, Milroy only succeeded in slowing himself when a rapid retreat would have undoubtedly been wiser. But neither Fremont nor Schenck nor Milroy fully comprehended the situation. They were measuring success by the accumulation of real estate, and they were reluctant to relinquish their accumulations. In fact, they stood to gain far more by retreat because Blenker was still coming, and Jackson would be drawn ever farther away from the Shenandoah and Richmond. But human nature prevailed, as Jackson seemed to know it would, and Schenck marched to Milroy, rather than Milroy to Schenck.

On 8 May, Johnson, with Jackson's map maker, Jedediah Hotchkiss, to guide him, soon veered south of the Parkersburg-Staunton road and through dense underbrush to the tangled top of Sitlington's Hill. Below them, just across the Bull Pasture River in McDowell, stood the combined commands of Milroy and Schenck. The Federals were sitting ducks, or so the Federals thought. What they did not know was that the Confederate artillery could not get through the undergrowth to the hill. So, when Jackson came up, he and Johnson could see their prey, but they could not strike them, at least not from Sitlington's Hill. The Southerners would have to make a river assault, so Jackson and Hotchkiss looked north for a vulnerable flank.

But Schenck, the senior Federal brigadier on the field saw only his own vulnerability and none of the Confederate difficulties in exploiting it. Therefore, extrication became his primary concern, and, since his force was about the same size as Johnson's, he approved Milroy's plan to launch a preemptive attack to buy time until nightfall. But what they bought only benefited the Confederates because their attack allowed Jackson's troops time to finally catch up with Johnson's. The Federals could have retreated with relative safety at any time during the day. Instead, their bold, but unecessary uphill attack was launched in the afternoon. It achieved some surprise — it never had a chance of achieving anything else.

Johnson's men were not in a defensive or fortified posture, and his right was soon threatened, so Jackson sent help. Then the center was assaulted, and the Southerners proved they were not immune to the human tendency for foolish bravery. The men of the 12th Georgia Regiment, the only non-Virginians of the Southerners there, were intent upon proving their worth. They stood up to fire down on their attackers, but in so doing, silhouetted themselves against the sky, and the result was devastating — a third of all Confederate casualties that day came from their ranks.

Brig. Gen. Taliaferro commanded the reinforcements from Jackson, and he soon commanded on the field as well, for Johnson fell with a painful ankle wound. At the time, Jackson was striving to find a way to flank the Federal left and also for a way to get his guns into action. Simultaneously, he was shuttling troops into the fight, but at no time did Jackson actually direct the battle.

Just as Richmond had its chain of command problems, so too, Jackson had his, and it plagued his tactical performance throughout the campaign. At Kernstown, his command consisted of only his own division, but that changed at McDowell when Johnson's division joined his forces. At this point, Jackson should have replaced himself as a division commander, but he did not. Instead, in addition to Johnson, the commanders of his own division's artillery, cavalry (though Ashby was absent) and three brigades continued to report directly to him. Later, when Jackson linked up with Ewell, Johnson's division would be absorbed into Ewell's, but this only meant that Ewell replaced the wounded Johnson in the chain of command. Throughout the campaign, Jackson remained both an army and a division commander.

Several possible reasons existed for this unwieldy command structure, including perhaps: Jackson's obvious reluctance to give up control of his own division; the idea that Jackson may have wished to assert more tactical impact than would have been afforded him by only controlling two divisions; but the most likely reason was one of propriety. Jackson was officially only in command of his own division, and it was part of Gen. J.E. Johnston's army. This status never changed, yet as Johnston became more embroiled on the Peninsula against McClellan, Jackson, with Lee's obvious approval, became increasingly independent, and the Valley Army became a reality if not a fact. So propriety precluded Jackson from replacing himself as commander of his old division, and tactics if not strategy suffered as a result.

These same reasons of propriety brought recently promoted Brig. Gen. Taliaferro, the commander of a brigade, to command both Confederate divisions on Sitlington's Hill. It was Johnson's show, and when he fell, Taliaferro was the only other general on the hill.

Only a few months earlier, before the Valley Campaign had commenced, Taliaferro had been among the officers to protest Jackson's generalship directly to Richmond. In the end, neither man had wanted to serve with the other, but both were overruled. Taliaferro had much to redeem, and at McDowell he did so, driving off the Federal attacks before Jackson came up at 9 p.m.

THE COST

Confederate: 75 killed, 423 wounded, 0 missing — total 498.
Federal: 26 killed, 227 wounded, 3 missing —total 256.

The Federals recrossed the river and slipped out of McDowell during the night. The following day, Jackson's men took up the pursuit although Schenck's soldiers set forest fires to slow them. Still the Confederates persisted until they reached a point just south of Franklin. Simultaneously, Hotchkiss and a cavalry contingent were off blocking many of the Shenandoah Mountain passes (North River, Dry River and Brock's Gaps) with boulders and felled trees. In this way, Fremont and Banks were significantly separated. Jackson had accomplished all that he could for this "Fremont" phase of operations. This was well, for on 13 May, Gen. Johnston let Gen. Lee know of his displeasure at being bypassed, and he ordered Jackson to return to the Valley.

By then, too, Ewell was certain Jackson was a "crazy man," a view with which Johnston apparently sympathized if not concurred. This was also all to the good, for if Jackson's friends did not understand his strategy, then certainly neither did his enemies. For the time being, it was unperceived brilliance, which in war is the best kind.

IX. THE BATTLE OF FRONT ROYAL

"I knew it must be Stonewall, when I heard the first gun. Go back quick and tell him that the Yankee force is very small — one regiment of Maryland infantry, several pieces of artillery and several companies of cavalry. Tell him I know, for I went through the camps and got it out of an officer. Tell him to charge right down and he will catch them all. I must hurry back. Good-by. My love to all the dear boys — and remember if you meet me in town you haven't seen me today."
— Belle Boyd

It was mid-May in the second year of war, and women were plowing up the fertile Shenandoah soil to plant seeds or place loved ones. Few Southerners then realized it, but the Shenandoah was holding the hopes of the South.

Stonewall Jackson had just won a battle at McDowell, but it was, after all, a little victory, and therefore little comfort as Gen. McClellan's massive Federal Army of the Potomac swarmed like locusts up the Peninsula toward Richmond. It was little comfort as Gen. McDowell's overwhelming numbers prepared once again to march on Richmond from Fredericksburg. In fact, if Jackson wanted a little victory in the mountains west of the Valley, the Federals would not begrudge it. Jackson could play in his Valley because the Federals had the real work of war to conduct before Richmond.

Northern disdain of Jackson's victory was matched by Southern indifference, and in the case of Brig. Gen. Ewell, down right ridicule: "I was ordered here (Swift Run Gap) to support General Jackson, pressed by Banks. But he (Jackson), immediately upon my arrival, started on a long chase after a body of the enemy far above Staunton... Jackson wants me to watch Banks. At Richmond, they want me everywhere and call me off, when, at the same time, I am compelled to remain until that enthusiastic fanatic (Jackson) comes to some conclusion.''

Never was the Confederate chain of command more disruptive. In April, Johnston was far down the Peninsula at Yorktown, so he communicated very little with his subordinates Jackson and Ewell. It was a void filled by Robert E. Lee, and Johnston made only minimal protests — in April. But in May, Johnston and his army were at Richmond. The Confederacy's dangers were therefore greater, and Johnston was then as near his subordinates as Lee was. Accordingly, Johnston reasserted control, and his instructions flowed, especially to Ewell. Meanwhile, Lee's orders and Jackson's ''requests'' to Ewell continued unabated. In just over two weeks, Ewell received 27 dispatches from Lee, Johnston and Jackson, and this correspondence contained some of the most fascinating and contradictory orders to come out of the Civil War — or any other war. It is a study in delicate confusion, at once both an example of disunified command and of a subordinate's (Jackson) singlemindedness of purpose. Most of all, Jackson provided a classic example of disobedience without insubordination.

13 May 1862, Johnston to Ewell:

''GENERAL: I have written to Major-General Jackson to return to the valley near you, and if your united force is strong enough, to attack General Banks.

''Should the latter cross the Blue Ridge to join General McDowell at Fredericksburg, General Jackson and yourself should move eastward rapidly...''

13 May 1862, Jackson to Ewell:

''If Banks goes down the valley I wish you to follow him...''

14 May 1862, Lee to Ewell:

''Unless Banks leaves the valley entirely, you must remain in present position until General Jackson's safe return is secured or until otherwise ordered.''

Johnston wanted Ewell east of the Valley (after Shields of Banks' command had moved east), Jackson wanted Ewell in the Valley, and Lee supported Jackson while trying to pacify Johnston. Meanwhile, Johnston was preparing to strike a blow at McClellan, and Jackson, enroute back to the Valley, was proceeding with his plans by manipulating the convoluted Confederate chain of command with calm coercion. Ewell, who was the foil in this gentlemanly, high-command fencing, was exasperated. Here he was ordered to cooperate with Jackson and also ordered to move east against Jackson's wishes. Aware of this, Jackson inundated Ewell not with orders or even requests, but rather with concepts, and eventually Jackson's concepts began to make more sense than Johnston's orders. Also, Lee's nudging weighed heavily on Ewell — though it should be remembered that Lee was not then held in the same high esteem he would later hold.

Ewell could simply have followed Johnston's orders, but by then the chain of command, as it concerned the Shenandoah, was breaking down, and it had become clear that Jackson was Ewell's commander in unofficial fact if not in official form — Ewell could read between the lines as well as any man and there was no longer any doubt that Richmond (Davis and Lee) wanted him to do so. He rode to Jackson.

Ewell met with Jackson at Mount Solon on 18 May, and it was there that Jackson won the balance of the campaign with both political cunning and military brilliance. His brillance provided the reason and his cunning provided the means, and that day, he provided Ewell with an order that was as ingenious as his campaign. :

"GENERAL: Your letter of this date, in which you state that you have received letters from Generals Lee, Johnston, and myself requiring somewhat different movements, and desiring my views respecting your position, has been received (in person). In reply I would state that as you are in the Valley District you constitute part of my command. Should you receive orders different from those sent from these headquarters, please advise me of the same at as early a period as practicable.

"You will please move your command so as to encamp between New Market and Mount Jackson on next Wednesday night, unless you receive orders from a superior officer and of a date subsequent to the 16th instant."

With propriety and disobedience established, Jackson reorganized the Valley Army by incorporating Edward Johnson's men into Ewell's division. He would have been better served by appointing commanders for his own as well as Johnson's division. In that way Jackson would have had, including Ewell's, three infantry divisions plus artillery plus Ashby's cavalry under his direct command. It would have been a command structure that could only have benefited the army's tactical performance, but it was not to be.

At this time, Fremont's men were licking their wounds in their now isolated positions west of Shenandoah Mountain; Shields' division had joined McDowell at Fredericksburg; and the bulk of Banks' depleted force was entrenched at Strasburg. The balance of Banks' troops, 1000 men under Col. John Kenly, were at Front Royal guarding the northern end of Luray Valley.

Then, as it became clear that the portion of Banks' command under Shields had left the Valley for Fredericksburg, the Confederate contradictions widened:

17 May 1862, Johnston to Ewell:
"GENERAL: If Banks is fortifying near Strasburg the attack would be too hazardous. In such an event we must leave him in his works. General Jackson can observe him and you come eastward....

"After reading this send it to General Jackson, for whom it is intended as well as yourself."

For the moment, Ewell obeyed only the last part of these orders, and once again departed for a meeting with Jackson. Jackson was pleased to see him, but Ewell replied, "You will not be so glad when I tell you what brought me."

"What — are the Yankees after you?" Jackson joked.

"Worse than that," replied an unsmiling Ewell. "I am ordered to join General Johnston."

All of Jackson's plans and marching and fighting and manipulating were on the verge of vanishing. He quickly fired off a plea to Gen. Lee:

"CAMP NEAR NEW MARKET, VA.,
May 20, 1862.

General R.E. Lee:

I am of opinion that an attempt should be made to defeat Banks, but under instructions just received from General Johnston I do not feel at liberty to make an attack. Please answer by telegraph at once.
T.J. JACKSON,
Major-General"

Neither Lee nor Johnston ever recorded what transpired between them as a result of Jackson's plea, but the next day, 21 May 1862, Johnston sent Jackson a cable:

"If you and Ewell united can beat Banks do it. I cannot judge at this distance. My previous instructions warned you against attacking fortifications. If it is not feasible to attack let Genl Ewell march toward Hanover C.H. Reporting from time to time on his way. Only general instructions can be given at this distance."

In 24 hours Stonewall Jackson's fortunes, and collaterally the South's fortunes, were first dashed then reversed. In that time, Jackson's combination of action, insubordination and intrigue had catapulted him from a division commander in Johnston's army into the commanding general of the offensively viable Valley Army, a position that would finally give a latitude of independence sufficient for his genius to thrive. Until 21 May, Jackson had been compelled to operate under the Confederate chain of command handicaps — a fact which made his accomplishments until then all

Lt. Gen.
Thomas J. "Stonewall" Jackson, C.S.A.

V.M.I. Professor
Thomas J. "Old Blue Light" Jackson

Jackson's beloved wife, Anna

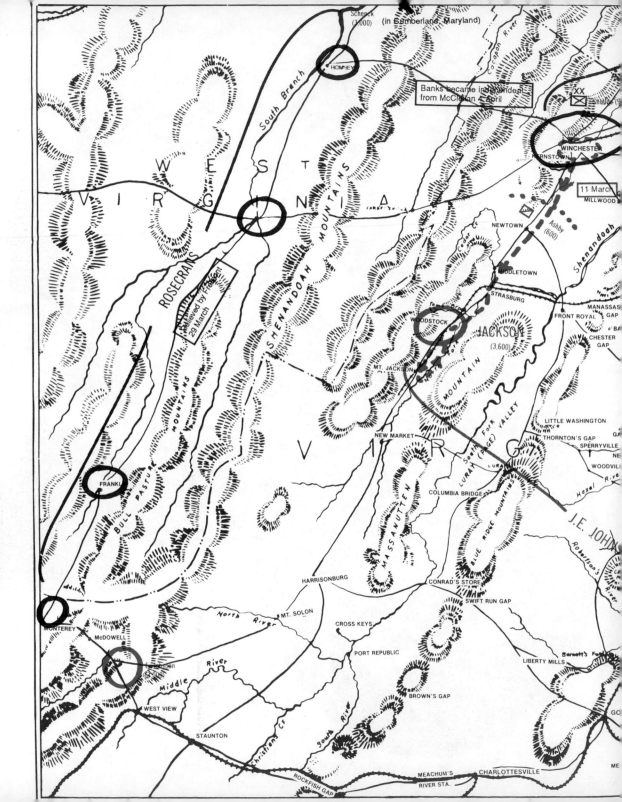

Schenck
(3,000) (in Cumberland, Maryland)

ROMNEY

South Branch

Potomac River

W E S T

Banks became independent
from McClellan 4 April

XX
Banks (9,000)

WINCHESTER

KERNSTOWN

11 March

MILLWOOD

Ashby
(600)

V I R G I N I A

NEWTOWN

MIDDLETOWN

Cedar Creek

Shenandoah

ROSECRANS

Relieved by Fremont
29 March

MANASSAS GAP

STRASBURG

FRONT ROYAL

o BA

WOODSTOCK

JACKSON
(3,600)

CHESTER GAP

MT. JACKSON

North Fork

MASSANUTTEN MOUNTAIN

NEW MARKET

FRANKLIN

BULL PASTURE MOUNTAINS

South Fork (PAGE) VALLEY

LITTLE WASHINGTON

THORNTON'S GAP

SPERRYVILLE

NE

LURAY

WOODVILL

COLUMBIA BRIDGE

Hazel River

BLUE RIDGE MOUNTAINS

J. E. JOHN

North River

MT. SOLON

Robertson's

HARRISONBURG

CONRAD'S STORE

SWIFT RUN GAP

MONTEREY

McDOWELL

Middle River

CROSS KEYS

LIBERTY MILLS

Bernett's Fo

F. Johnson
(3,000)

PORT REPUBLIC

WEST VIEW

BROWN'S GAP

STAUNTON

Christians Cr

South River

GO

ME

MEACHUM'S
RIVER STA.

CHARLOTTESVILLE

ROCKFISH GAP

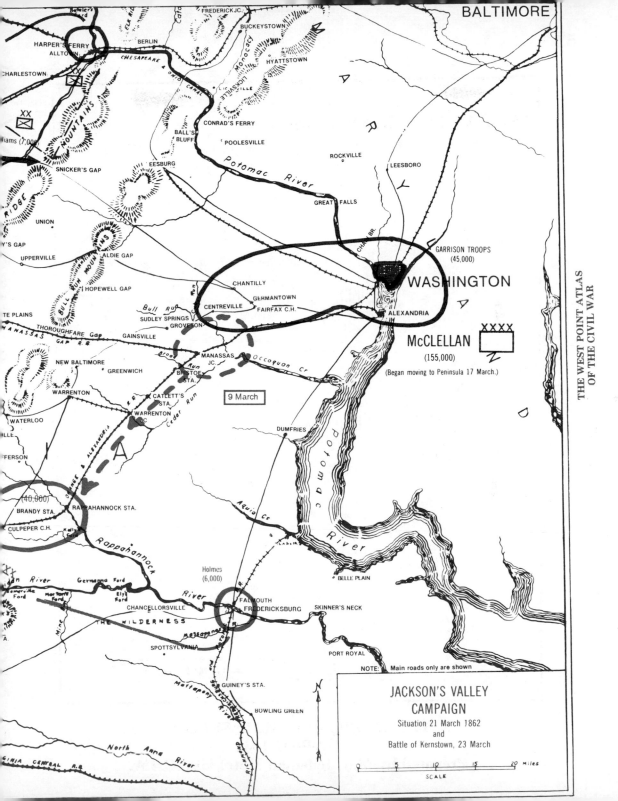

BALTIMORE

THE WEST POINT ATLAS
OF THE CIVIL WAR

GARRISON TROOPS
(45,000)

WASHINGTON

McCLELLAN

(155,000)

(Began moving to Peninsula 17 March.)

9 March

Williams (7,000)

HARPER'S FERRY
ALLTOWN

CHARLESTOWN

SNICKER'S GAP

UNION

UPPERVILLE

ALDIE GAP

HOPEWELL GAP

TE PLAINS

THOROUGHFARE Gap

GAINSVILLE

NEW BALTIMORE

GREENWICH

WARRENTON

WATERLOO

lle

fferson

(40,000)

BRANDY STA.

CULPEPER C.H.

RAPPAHANNOCK STA.

Rappahannock River

Germanna Ford

Ely's Ford

CHANCELLORSVILLE

THE WILDERNESS

SPOTTSYLVANIA

BERLIN

FREDERICK JC.

BUCKEYSTOWN

HYATTSTOWN

CONRAD'S FERRY

BALL'S BLUFF

POOLESVILLE

ROCKVILLE

LEESBORO

Potomac River

GREAT FALLS

EESBURG

CHANTILLY

GERMANTOWN

CENTREVILLE

FAIRFAX C.H.

ALEXANDRIA

SUDLEY SPRINGS

GROVETON

MANASSAS JC.

Occoquan Cr

BRISTOE STA.

CATLETT'S STA.

WARRENTON JC.

Cedar Run

DUMFRIES

Aquia Cr

BELLE PLAIN

Holmes
(6,000)

FALMOUTH

FREDERICKSBURG

SKINNER'S NECK

PORT ROYAL

GUINEY'S STA.

BOWLING GREEN

North Anna River

NOTE: Main roads only are shown

JACKSON'S VALLEY
CAMPAIGN

Situation 21 March 1862
and
Battle of Kernstown, 23 March

0   5   10   15   20 Miles
SCALE

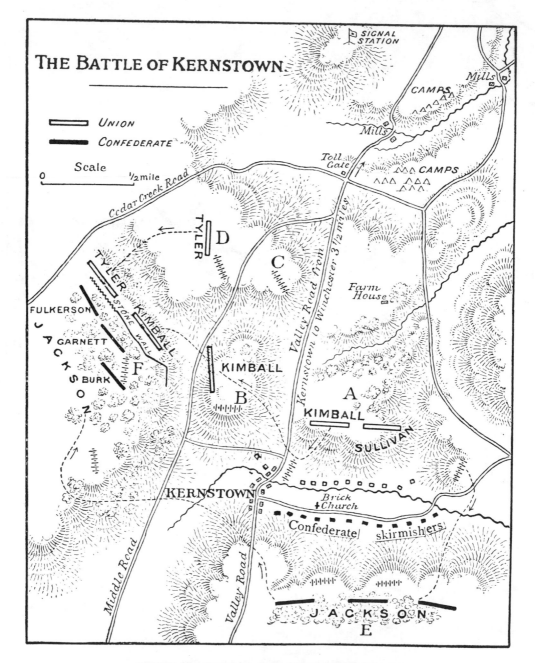

THE BATTLE OF KERNSTOWN
23 MARCH 1862
Prepared by Maj. Jedediah Hotchkiss, C.S.A.

Maj. Gen. Nathan Kimball, U.S.V.
Courtesy Battles and Leaders

Brig. Gen. Turner Ashby, C.S.A.

Brig. Gen. Richard B. Garnett, C.S.A.

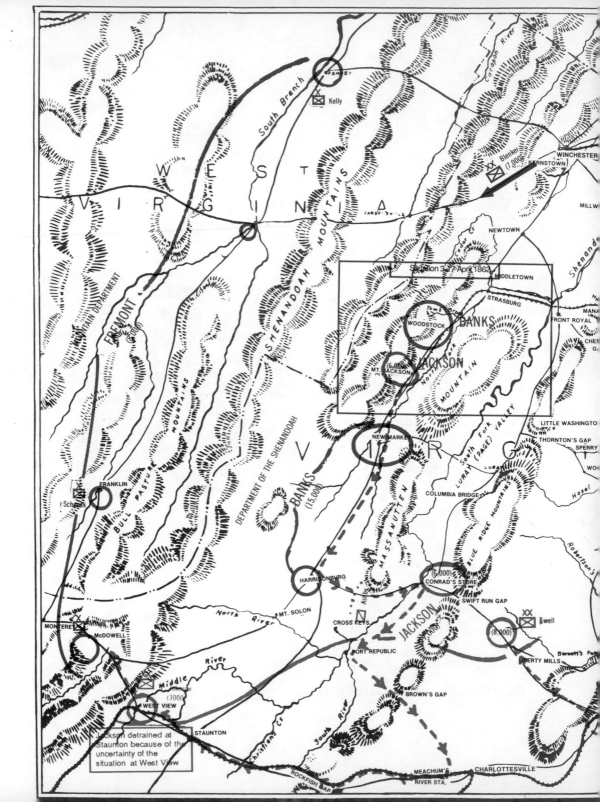

Situation 3-17 April 1862

Jackson detrained at Staunton because of the uncertainty of the situation at West View

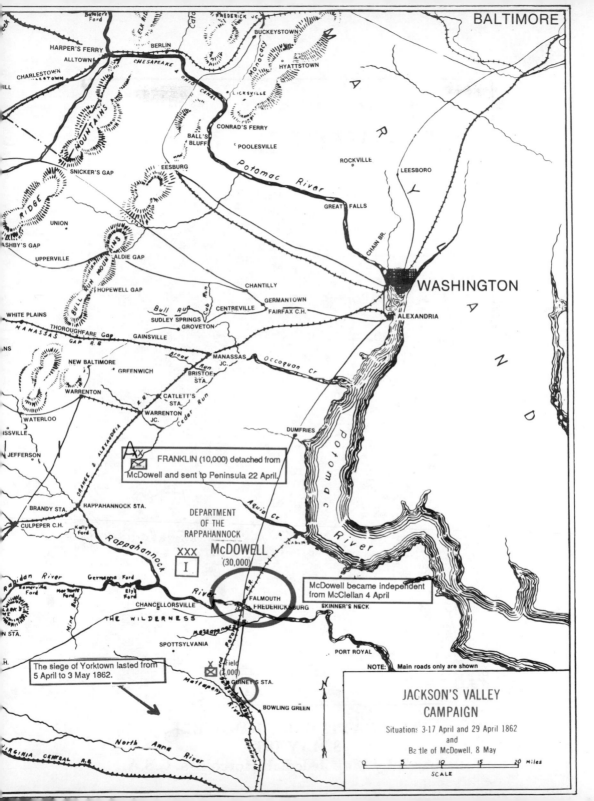

BALTIMORE

THE WEST POINT ATLAS
OF THE CIVIL WAR

HARPER'S FERRY
ALLTOWN
CHARLESTOWN
CHESAPEAKE & OHIO CANAL
BERLIN
FREDERICK JC.
BUCKEYSTOWN
HYATTSTOWN
LICKSVILLE
CONRAD'S FERRY
BALL'S BLUFF
POOLESVILLE
ROCKVILLE
LEESBORO
SNICKER'S GAP
EESBURG
Potomac River
GREAT FALLS
UNION
ASHBY'S GAP
UPPERVILLE
CHAIN BR.
WASHINGTON
ALDIE GAP
CHANTILLY
GERMANTOWN
HOPEWELL GAP
ALEXANDRIA
WHITE PLAINS
Bull Run
Cub Run
CENTREVILLE
FAIRFAX C.H.
SUDLEY SPRINGS
GROVETON
THOROUGHFARE GAP
MANASSAS GAP R.R.
GAINSVILLE
NEW BALTIMORE
GREENWICH
Broad Run
MANASSAS JC.
Occoquan Cr.
BRISTOE STA.
WARRENTON
CATLETT'S STA.
WARRENTON JC.
Cedar Run
WATERLOO
DUMFRIES
JEFFERSON

FRANKLIN (10,000) detached from
McDowell and sent to Peninsula 22 April.

BRANDY STA.
RAPPAHANNOCK STA.
Aquia Cr.
CULPEPER C.H.
Kelly Ford
Rappahannock
River

DEPARTMENT
OF THE
RAPPAHANNOCK

XXX
I
McDOWELL
(30,000)

McDowell became independent
from McClellan 4 April

Rapidan River
Germanna Ford
Somerville Ford
Morton's Ford
Elk's Ford
FALMOUTH
FREDERICKSBURG
SKINNER'S NECK
CHANCELLORSVILLE
THE WILDERNESS
SPOTTSYLVANIA
PORT ROYAL

The siege of Yorktown lasted from
5 April to 3 May 1862.

field
(1,000)
GUINEY'S STA.
Mattapony River
BOWLING GREEN

NOTE: Main roads only are shown

N

JACKSON'S VALLEY
CAMPAIGN

Situations 3-17 April and 29 April 1862
and
Battle of McDowell, 8 May

0   5   10   15   20 Miles
SCALE

North Anna River
VIRGINIA CENTRAL R.R.
RICHMOND

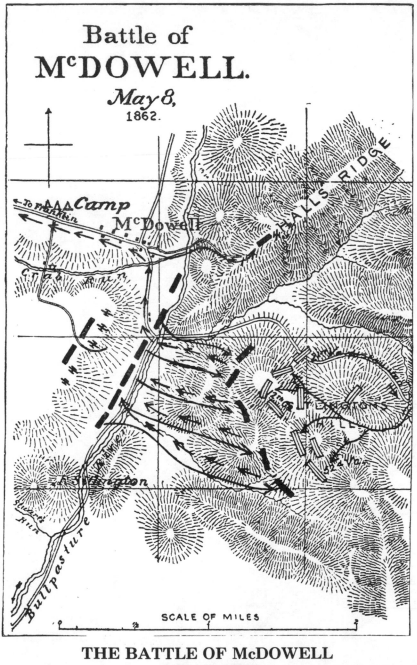

THE BATTLE OF McDOWELL
8 MAY 1862
Prepared by Maj. Jedediah Hotchkiss, C.S.A.

Maj. Gen. Edward Johnson, C.S.A.

Brig. Gen. William B. Taliaferro, C.S.A.

Brig. Gen. Robert Milroy, U.S.V.   Maj. Gen. Robert Schenck, U.S.V.

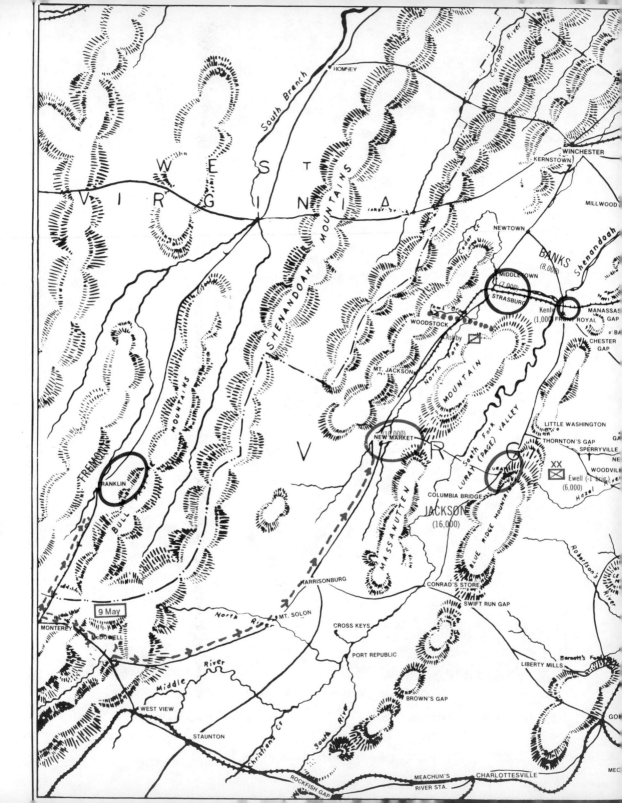

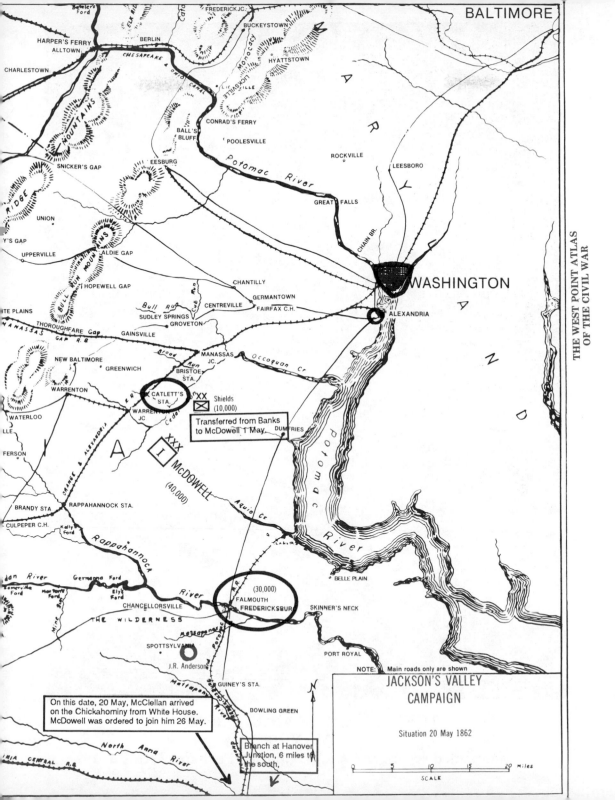

THE WEST POINT ATLAS
OF THE CIVIL WAR

HARPER'S FERRY
ALLTOWN
BERLIN
CHARLESTOWN
CHESAPEAKE & OHIO CANAL
MOUNTAINS
SNICKER'S GAP
EESBURG
BALL'S BLUFF
UNION
Y'S GAP
UPPERVILLE
ALDIE GAP

FREDERICK JC.
BUCKEYSTOWN
HYATTSTOWN
CONRAD'S FERRY
POOLESVILLE
ROCKVILLE
LEESBORO
Potomac River
GREAT FALLS
CHAIN BR.
WASHINGTON
ALEXANDRIA

CHANTILLY
GERMANTOWN
HOPEWELL GAP
Bull Run
CENTREVILLE
FAIRFAX C.H.
TE PLAINS
SUDLEY SPRINGS
GROVETON
THOROUGHFARE Gap
MANASSAS GAP R.R.
GAINSVILLE
Broad
MANASSAS JC.
Occoquan Cr.
NEW BALTIMORE
GREENWICH
BRISTOE STA.
Run
WARRENTON
CATLETT'S STA.
WATERLOO
WARRENTON JC.
Cedar
LLE
FERSON

XX Shields (10,000)

Transferred from Banks to McDowell 1 May.

DUMFRIES

XXX I McDOWELL (40,000)

A

BRANDY STA.
RAPPAHANNOCK STA.
CULPEPER C.H.
Kelly Ford
Rappahannock
River
dan River
Germanna Ford
Somerville Ford
Mot Ton's Ford
Ely's Ford
CHANCELLORSVILLE
THE WILDERNESS
SPOTTSYLVANIA
J.R. ANDERSON
North Anna River
RIA CENTRAL R.R.

Aquia Cr.

BELLE PLAIN

(30,000)
FALMOUTH
FREDERICKSBURG
SKINNER'S NECK

PORT ROYAL

GUINEY'S STA.
BOWLING GREEN
Mattapony

On this date, 20 May, McClellan arrived on the Chickahominy from White House. McDowell was ordered to join him 26 May.

Branch at Hanover Junction, 6 miles to the south.

NOTE: Main roads only are shown

JACKSON'S VALLEY
CAMPAIGN

Situation 20 May 1862

0   5   10   15   20 Miles
SCALE

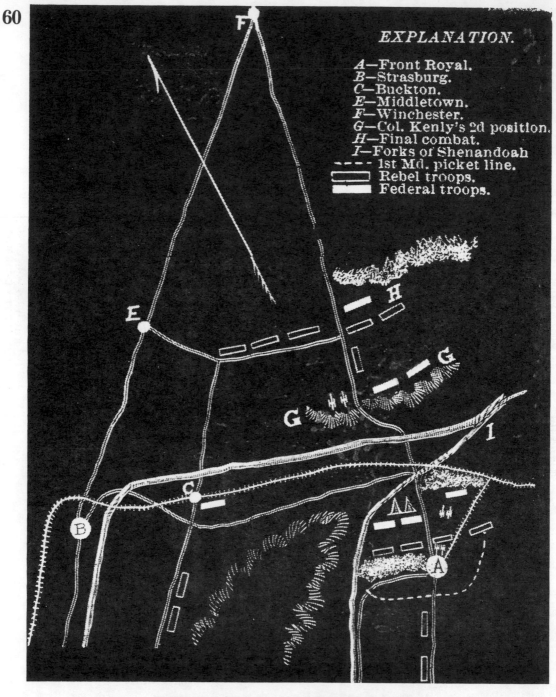

EXPLANATION.

A—Front Royal.
B—Strasburg.
C—Buckton.
E—Middletown.
F—Winchester.
G—Col. Kenly's 2d position.
H—Final combat.
I—Forks of Shenandoah
- - - - 1st Md. picket line.
Rebel troops.
Federal troops.

THE BATTLE OF FRONT ROYAL
23 MAY 1862
Accompanied report of Lt. Col. Charles Parham, 29th Pa. Inf.

Miss Belle Boyd, spy

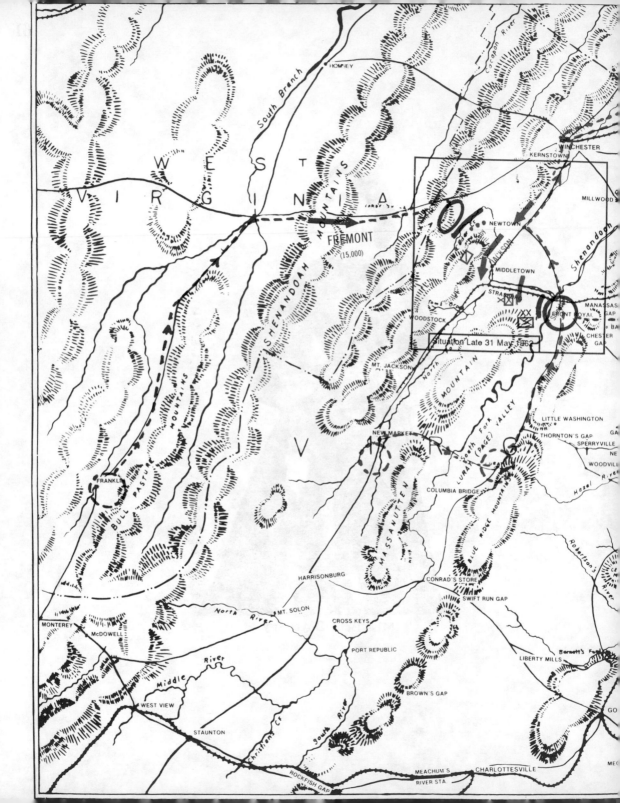

Situation Late 31 May 1862

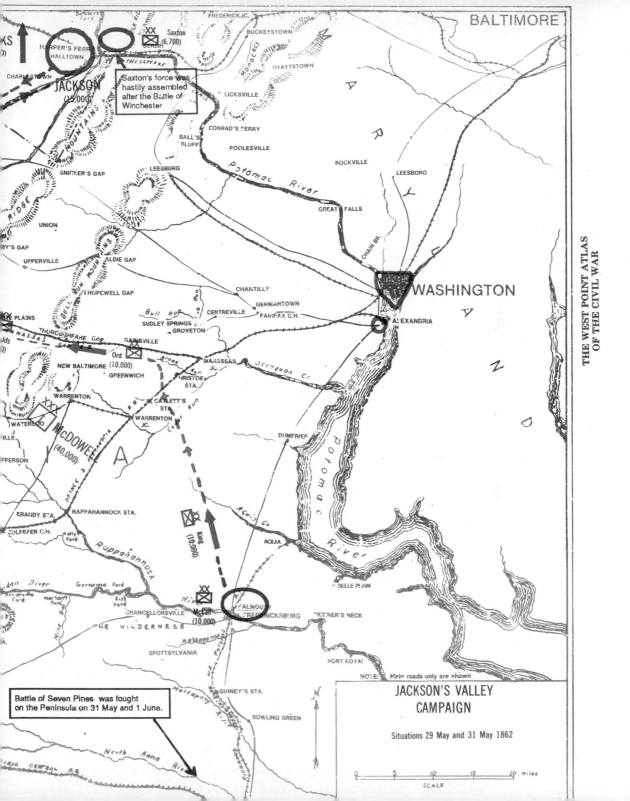

BALTIMORE

FREDERICK JC.
BUCKEYSTOWN

XX Saxton
Berlin (6,700)

HARPER'S FERRY
HALLTOWN

CHESAPEAKE

CHARLESTOWN

JACKSON
(15,000)

Saxton's force was
hastily assembled
after the Battle of
Winchester

HYATTSTOWN

LICKSVILLE

CONRAD'S FERRY

BALL'S
BLUFF

POOLESVILLE

ROCKVILLE

SNICKER'S GAP

LEESBORO

UNION

LEESBURG

Potomac River

GREAT FALLS

BY'S GAP

UPPERVILLE

ALDIE GAP

CHAIN BR.

WASHINGTON

HOPEWELL GAP

CHANTILLY

GERMANTOWN

Bull Run

SUDLEY SPRINGS

CENTREVILLE

FAIRFAX C.H.

ALEXANDRIA

E PLAINS

GROVETON

THOROUGHFARE GAP

Ord
(10,000)

GAINSVILLE

MANASSAS
JC.

Occoquan Cr.

NEW BALTIMORE

GREENWICH

BRISTOE
STA.

WARRENTON

CATLETT'S
STA.

XX
McDOWELL
(40,000)

WATERLOO

WARRENTON
JC.

DUMFRIES

FFERSON

BRANDY STA.

RAPPAHANNOCK STA.

CULPEPER C.H.

Kelly
Ford

Rappahannock River

XX King
(10,000)

AQUIA

BELLE PLAIN

dan River

Germanna Ford

MacKay's
Ford

CHANCELLORSVILLE

XX
McCall
(10,000)

FALMOUTH
FREDERICKSBURG

SKINNER'S NECK

THE WILDERNESS

SPOTTSYLVANIA

PORT ROYAL

Battle of Seven Pines was fought
on the Peninsula on 31 May and 1 June.

GUINEY'S STA.

BOWLING GREEN

NOTE: Main roads only are shown

N

JACKSON'S VALLEY
CAMPAIGN

Situations 29 May and 31 May 1862

North Anna River

0   5   10   15   20 Miles

SCALE

THE WEST POINT ATLAS
OF THE CIVIL WAR

64

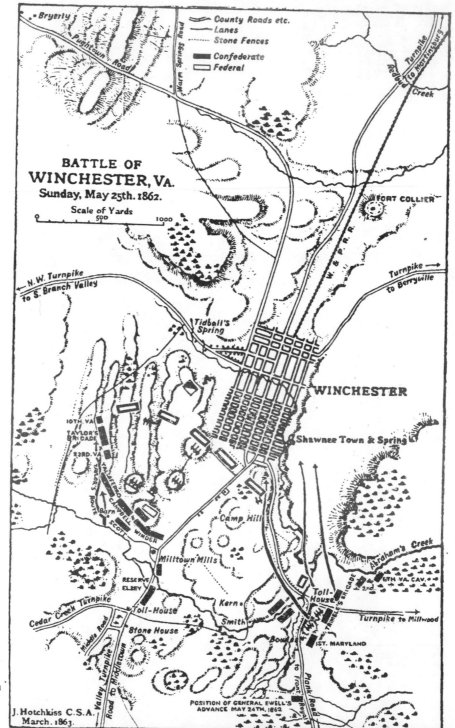

clarifications
by D.A. Cohn

Lt. Gen. Richard Taylor, C.S.A.

Jackson's "Foot Cavalry"

Courtesy Battles and Leaders

Maj. Gen. Nathaniel "Napoleon" P. Banks, U.S.V.

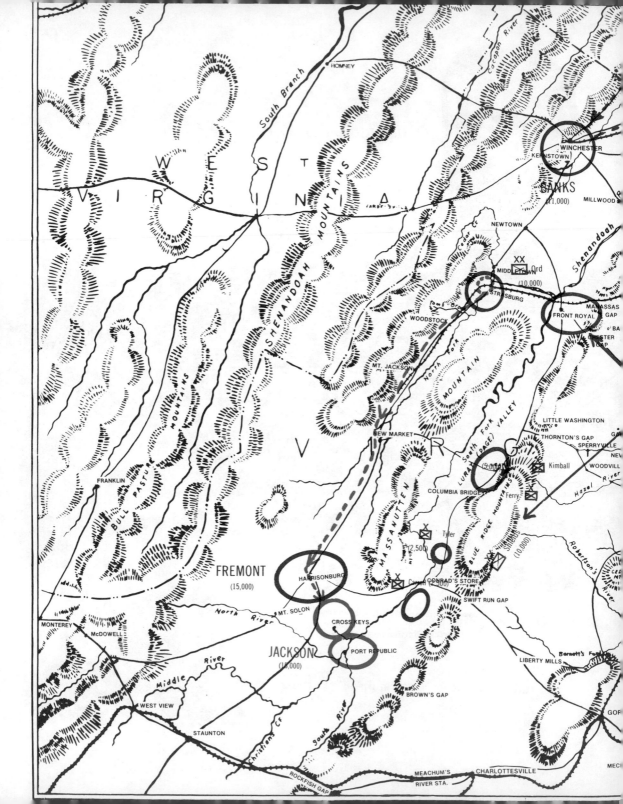

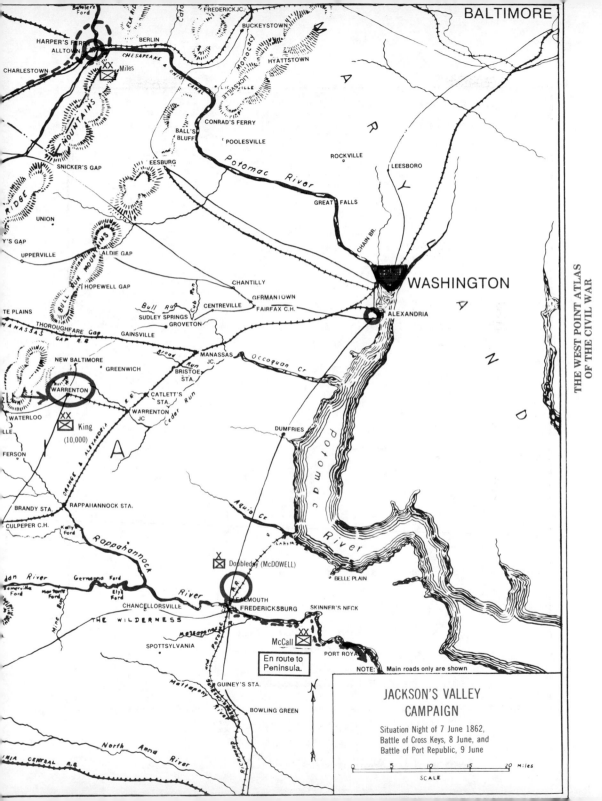

BALTIMORE

THE WEST POINT ATLAS
OF THE CIVIL WAR

FREDERICK JC.
BUCKEYSTOWN
HYATTSTOWN
HARPER'S FERRY
ALLTOWN
BERLIN
CHESAPEAKE & OHIO CANAL
CHARLESTOWN
XX Miles
MOUNTAINS
CONRAD'S FERRY
CONRAD'S FERRY
BALL'S
BLUFF
POOLESVILLE
ROCKVILLE
LEESBORO
SNICKER'S GAP
EESBURG
Potomac River
GREAT FALLS
RIDGE
UNION
CHAIN BR.
Y'S GAP
ALDIE GAP
UPPERVILLE
HOPEWELL GAP
CHANTILLY
WASHINGTON
GERMANTOWN
Bull Run
CENTREVILLE
FAIRFAX C.H.
ALEXANDRIA
TE PLAINS
THOROUGHFARE Gap
SUDLEY SPRINGS
GROVETON
GAINSVILLE
MANASSAS GAP R.R.
NEW BALTIMORE
GREENWICH
MANASSAS
JC.
Occoquan Cr.
BRISTOE
STA.
WARRENTON
CATLETT'S
STA.
WATERLOO
XX King
(10,000)
WARRENTON
JC.
Cedar Run
DUMFRIES
FERSON
ORANGE & ALEXANDRIA R.R.
BRANDY STA.
RAPPAHANNOCK STA.
Aquia Cr.
CULPEPER C.H.
Kelly
Ford
Rappahannock
River
Doubleday (McDOWELL)
BELLE PLAIN
dan River
Germanna Ford
Somerville
Ford
Mott's
Ford
Ely's
Ford
River
FALMOUTH
FREDERICKSBURG
SKINNER'S NECK
CHANCELLORSVILLE
THE WILDERNESS
McCall XX
SPOTTSYLVANIA
PORT ROYAL
En route to
Peninsula.
NOTE: Main roads only are shown
GUINEY'S STA.
N
JACKSON'S VALLEY
CAMPAIGN
BOWLING GREEN
Situation Night of 7 June 1862,
Battle of Cross Keys, 8 June, and
Battle of Port Republic, 9 June
VIRGINIA CENTRAL R.R.
North Anna River
0   5   10   15   20 Miles
SCALE

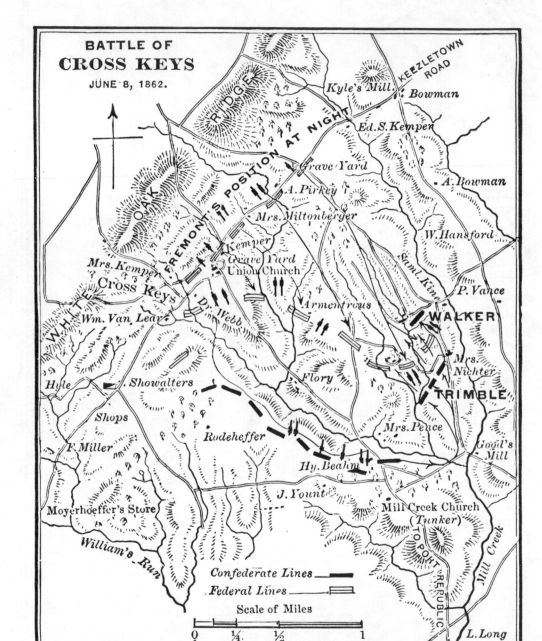

THE BATTLE OF CROSS KEYS
8 JUNE 1862
Prepared by Maj. Jedediah Hotchkiss, C.S.A.

Lt. Gen.
Richard S. Ewell, C.S.A.

Maj. Gen.
John C. Fremont, U.S.V.

Brig. Gen.
Louis Blenker and staff

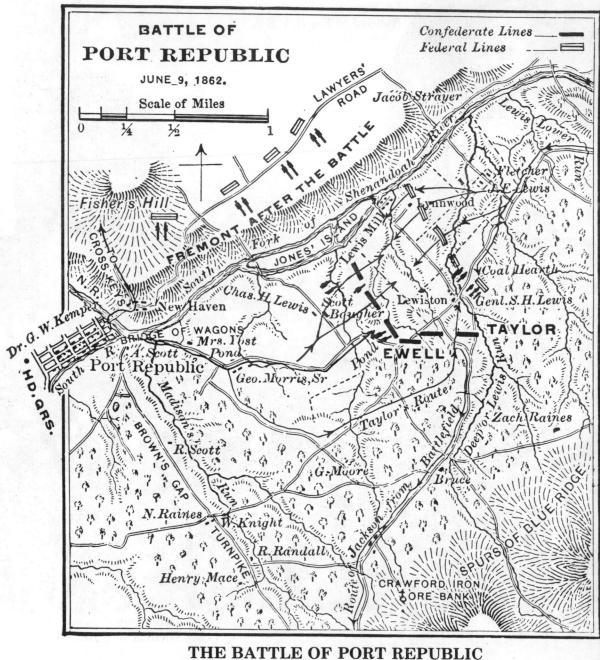

**THE BATTLE OF PORT REPUBLIC
9 JUNE 1862
Prepared by Maj. Jedediah Hotchkiss, C.S.A.**

**Brig. Gen.
Charles S. Winder, C.S.A.**
Courtesy Library of Congress

**Brig. Gen.
James Shields, U.S.V.**

Gen. Joseph E. Johnston,

Maj. Gen.
George B. McClellan,
U.S.V.

Courtesy Library of Congress

Courtesy National Archives

Gen. Robert E. Lee, C.S.A.

Maj. W.J. Hawks
Capt. J. Hotchkiss
Maj. (Dr.) H. McGuire

Maj. R.L. Dabney
Lt. Col. W. Allan
Lt. Col. A.S. Pendleton

Capt. J. Smith
Maj. H.K. Douglas

Capt. J.G. Morrison
Maj. D.B. Bridgeford

Jackson and his staff
Courtesy Library of Congress

the more remarkable. Now he was free, and events soon reflected it.

The 21st not only brought Johnston's cable, but Brig. Gen. Richard Taylor's 3,000 man brigade of Louisianans as well. They came from Ewell's division in accordance with Jackson's orders of the 19th in which Ewell was instructed to move his entire division from Swift Run Gap to Mount Jackson, north of New Market. But these orders and Taylor's march occurred during the height of the chain of command confusion. As a result, Taylor's was the only brigade to come from Ewell, and Jackson would treat it as a third division for the remainder of the campaign.

There still was no let up in orders. On the 20th, Brig. Gen. Branch's brigade, which had earlier been sent to Ewell by Lee, and which was then enroute to New Market, was suddenly ordered to a point north of Richmond by Johnston. Jackson then changed the instructions for the balance of Ewell's command, ordering it to remain in Luray Valley.

22 May, at "early dawn," as Jackson was inclined to say, saw his plans and army in synchronized motion. Ewell's division, less Taylor's brigade, was marching from Swift Run Gap north to Luray. West of Massanutten, Jackson and the rest of the Valley Army were also marching north, but at New Market, he turned it due east, also for Luray. Taylor, whose brigade was in the lead of Jackson's wing, wrote of his arrival in Luray:

"Here, after three long marches, we were but a short distance below the bridge at Conrad's Store (Elkton) — a point we had left several days before. I began to think Jackson was a concealed, perhaps unconscious poet, and, as an ardent lover of Nature, desired to give strangers an opportunity to admire the beauties of his Valley."

But Jackson was merely at his old game. Long marches to predictable points served to reinforce his enemies' preconceptions. Just as he had misled friend and foe alike by the earlier march out of the Valley to Meachum's River Station, so too had he done so by bringing Taylor to New Market.

Banks reported that same day from Strasburg, where his men were busily fortifying:

"The return of the rebel forces of General Jackson to the valley, after his forced march against Generals Milroy and Schenck, increases my anxiety . . .

"Once at New Market, they (Jackson and Ewell) are within 25 miles of Strasburg, with a force of not less than 16,000 men (Taylor's march had convinced him that all of Ewell's command had joined Jackson). My available force is between 4,000 and 5,000 infantry, 1,800 cavalry, and sixteen pieces of artillery. . . .

". . . our situation certainly invites attack in the strongest manner."

Banks had finally recognized the folly of sending Shields east. However, he failed to see the full extent of his own jeopardy, because what was true for him at Strasburg was even more so for Col. Kenly's 1,000 men at Front Royal. And Kenly was only a day away from disaster.

Banks, who had encouraged rather than protested the halving of his own command — the sending of Shields to Fredericksburg — was now complaining too late and about the wrong position. Still, the true Federal fault lay elsewhere. Lincoln was in command, and while he was reducing Banks' by Shields, he was reinforcing Fremont with Blenker. Then he compounded the error by allowing Fremont's army to languish west of the mountains, just as Banks' understrength force was desperately digging in at Strasburg.

On 23 May nearly 17,000 Confederates literally poured down Gooney Manor Road and descended upon the 1,000 Federals at Front Royal. It was then that the most famous of Confederate spies, Belle Boyd, raced under fire with messages for Stonewall.

Due to its nature, espionage is rarely well chronicled and is often well fictionalized—the exploits of Belle Boyd not being exempt. Yet, interestingly, in her case the facts proved to be more exciting than the fictions.

The high point of her career came at Front Royal that Stonewall spring of '62. Having just turned eighteen on 9 May, and not being particularly pretty, she was nonetheless known to have a "way" about her that caused gullible men to melt.

The prior year she had killed a Federal intruder at her parents' home in Martinsburg, and later she had been caught in the act of smuggling weapons and information to the Confederacy. Only her gender and age had saved her, and she was closely watched thereafter. Even so, she continued her activities, moved for a time to Front Royal, was arrested enroute back to Martinsburg, taken to Baltimore and released. Then her mother obtained Federal passes and escorted her once again to Front Royal. It was 12 May 1862.

Gen. Shields happened to be there at the time, enroute east with his division, and she sent him her card. The Federal general called on her for no other purpose than to engage in light-hearted banter with a beguiling spy whom he could not take seriously. But accompanying the general was his more impressionable aide-de-camp, Captain Daniel J. Keily, the famous "Captain K," whose name Belle Boyd never revealed. "To him," she wrote, "I am indebted for some very remarkable effusions, some withered flowers, and a great deal of important information." (He was later wounded at the Battle of Port Republic and brought back to Front Royal and Belle's care).

On the night of the 14 May, Shields held a council of war at the Fishback Hotel (later called the Strickler House). Someone had previously drilled a hole in the floor of an upstairs closet, and Belle proceeded to put it to good use. She heard all the Federal officers had to say, combined it with knowledge gained from "Captain K" and others, encoded it and was away in the night, riding through the lines to deliver the message to Col. Ashby.

Shortly thereafter, Shields and his 9,000 men departed for the east and were replaced by Col. Kenly's 1,000 man force: the 1st

Maryland, 29th Pennsylvania and 5th New York Cavalry.

Then, in the days before Jackson's arrival, she convinced a young Federal lieutenant to escort her to Winchester. There, a distinguished, but anonymous man gave her dispatches for Stonewall. On the return trip, however, she was given away and arrested. Interrogated, she confused and trivialized the issue by divulging a package of secessionist newspapers and implicating the Federal lieutenant in their acquisition. So the lieutenant was detained; she was not.

Her busy week climaxed with the arrival of Jackson's army before Front Royal. She heard the firing and ran outside where a racing Federal officer told her what was afoot and of Kenly's intention to burn the bridges (the railroad and road bridges over the South Fork and the road bridge over the North Fork). There she was with her Winchester dispatches still undelivered, with Kenly's dispositions well in mind and with the knowledge of Kenley's intent to burn the bridges and retreat rather than stand. The battle was developing around her, and she possessed information that could affect the outcome, so this teenage girl, alone in her purpose, let duty choose her course, and duty beckoned. This Confederate would convey her information. She raced between the lines toward the oncoming Southerners — her father among them as a private in the Stonewall Brigade. Federal artillery shells burst around her and bullets pierced her clothing, but she delivered her information to one of Jackson's aides, Henry Kyd Douglas.

To what extent her ride to Ashby, her Winchester dispatches and her verbal information assisted Stonewall is a matter of conjecture, but future Federal retribution and Confederate acclaim certainly implied that her contributions were significant indeed.

As Belle Boyd was delivering her information, the Valley Army was pressing ahead. Jackson had ordered up his Marylanders, knowing they wanted a go at what they considered the "bogus" 1st Maryland, US Volunteers. But Jackson had been unaware of the problems on the road behind him.

It was mid-May and mutiny was in the air. During the hard march back to the Valley following the victory at McDowell, none other than a portion of one regiment of the Stonewall Brigade had mutinied. With their twelve month enlistments up and the belief that the new Confederate conscription law was unfair, some men in the 27th Regiment had thrown down their arms and refused to go on. When their commander, Col. Grigsby, sent word of the incident to headquarters, Jackson roared, "What is this but mutiny? Why does Colonel Grigsby refer to me to know what to do with a mutiny? He should shoot them where they stand." Appropriate orders were issued, and the appropriate response was illicited: the men returned to the ranks. On that day they had faltered, but pride would compel fatal atonement for many of them in the battles to come.

Now, at Front Royal, as the call came for the gray lines to make way for their Marylanders, another mutiny was in the making. Many men in the 1st Maryland Regiment, C.S.A. had applied for transfer to the cavalry, but Jackson had insisted that all men remain in their original branches. As a result, and unknown to Jackson, about half of the 1st Maryland had mutinied and was being held under arrest by the other half when the order came: "Colonel Johnson will move the First Maryland to the front with all dispatch...."

Their commander and fellow Marylander, Col. (later Brig. Gen.) Bradley T. Johnson, complied by shaming them: "Boast of it when you meet your fathers and mothers, brothers, sisters and sweethearts. Tell them it was you who, when brought face to face with the enemy, proved yourselves... to be cowards."

But they were not cowards. The cavalry, not fear, had been their mutinous motivation, and they immediately responded to their colonel by shouldering their weapons and racing into harm's way to prove it.

In this way, the "Battle of Brothers" commenced. The 1st Maryland, C.S.A. charged down Gooney Manor Road into Front Royal and into the 1st Maryland, U.S. Volunteers, and at least one incident of a Confederate soldier capturing his Federal brother was recorded.

Due to the preponderance of numbers, the outcome was never in question, but the real question, as Belle Boyd pointed out, was one of bridges. Maj. Chatham Roberdeau Wheat's battalion of Louisiana Tigers from Taylor's brigade was with the 1st Maryland in the charge. Wheat, a soldier of fortune who had fought with Garibaldi in Italy and Walker in Nicaragua, was just the man to lead such a mix of men, including many of dubious reputations, who were as wild as they were bold. They demonstrated their wildness by "confiscating" a Federal supply train that stumbled into the battle, and they showed their boldness by following Stonewall Jackson and Gen. Taylor in their race under fire across the burning railroad bridge. This foiled Kenly's final attempt to stand on the north side of the North Fork.

Still, the day's work was not done. As Kenly's men sped for Winchester, all Jackson needed to complete the victory was artillery and cavalry, but Ashby had assigned an unreliable company for courier duty that day, and the young courier Jackson sent to order the guns up never delivered the message. Kenly was escaping.

Then, out of the dust and din of battle, Lt. Col. Thomas Flournoy and Companies A, B, E and K of the 6th Virginia Cavalry from Ewell's Division, 250 cavalrymen in all, suddenly appeared on Jackson's left. They had been on interdiction duty, cutting wires to the west of Front Royal, and that job complete, Flournoy, on his own initiative, had forded them across the North Fork. Now they and they alone, although outnumbered four to one, stood ready to pursue the fleeing Federals.

By the Civil War, weaponry had made cavalry charges against massed infantry impractical, but Flournoy's men stood as ready to do so as if they were the Light Brigade at Balaclava. A word from Jackson and they did just that. Catching the Federals just north of Front Royal at Cedarville, they charged with abandon, driving in the Federal cavalry. Kenly's infantry retreated and reformed, and Flournoy came on again in what Jackson described as "a second gallant and decisive charge" in which "the enemy's cavalry was put to flight, the artillery abandoned, and the infantry, now thrown into great confusion, surrendered themselves prisoners of war."

The Battle of Front Royal, however, was not an isolated event.

Rather it was part of a battle waged all across the Valley. Jackson was making every effort to confirm Banks' preconceptions, and this was accomplished by a Southern show of force from Strasburg to Front Royal. Ashby's troopers cut the wires and rails between those two points at Buckton. And as dusk approached on the 23rd, Capt. G. W. Myers and Capt. Edward MacDonald performed one of the almost forgotten, but crucial feints of the campaign when their small cavalry contingent occupied a hill just south of Strasburg. Their efforts were so convincing that Banks believed them to be Jackson's main force coming just as expected. So effective were Myers and MacDonald and so set in mind was Banks that he refused to believe the reports reaching him from Front Royal, believing the action there to be the feint.

THE COST

Confederate: 35 total casualties (they are included in the Battle of Winchester totals, Chapter X.)

Federal: 16 killed, 48 wounded, 689 missing — total 792 (including 39 unallocated casualties from the 5th New York Cavalry).

Note: Most sources erroneously show Federal casualties as 904 at Front Royal and 2,019 at Winchester which followed. The 904 figure came from Banks' initial estimate for both battles, which he soon after revised to 2,019. His official report indicated 792 of this number were lost at Front Royal, leaving 1,227 for Winchester and the skirmishes leading up to it. Banks also acknowledged leaving 1,189 men behind in hospitals, of which 1,000 had been left by Shields before his departure east. This would make the total Federal missing: 689 at Front Royal, 1,025 at Winchester and skirmishes, 1,189 in hospitals at Winchester and Strasburg for a total of 2,903 men. This compares to Jackson's estimate of 3,050, the difference probably being the hospital staffs which he released. All of the hospital captives were parolled.

The Battle of Front Royal cannot be measured in numbers because its significance far exceeded its size. Jackson said it best: "The fruits of this movement were not restricted to the stores and prisoners captured; the enemy's flank was turned and the road opened to Winchester." It was a breakthrough.

X. THE BATTLE OF WINCHESTER

"My God! Don't you love your country?"
—Maj. Gen. Nathaniel Banks, USV

"Yes, and I'm trying to get back to it as fast as I can."
—A retreating Federal soldier

The Federals lost Front Royal on 23 May, but Gen. Banks and his men remained steadfastly at Strasburg. They remained despite the reports. They remained without a plan. But Jackson did not know this. He assumed his enemies, like he, always had plans.

Banks waited, and dispatches continued coming in. Capt. Saville, a survivor of the 1st Maryland, USV, sent word: "Regiment cut all to pieces and prisoners . . . The enemy's forces are 15,000 or 20,000 strong, and on the march to Strasburg."

Banks forwarded the report to Secretary of War Stanton and followed it up with an assessment: "I deem it much overestimated . . ."

Later on the 23rd or early on the 24th, another Banks to Stanton dispatch read: "The enemy's force estimated at 5,000 or 6,000. It is reported as fallen back on Front Royal . . ."

Even on the morning of the 24th, his delusions continued: "The force of the enemy [at Front Royal] was very large; not less than 6,000 to 10,000. It is probably Ewell's force, passing through the Shenandoah Valley. Jackson is still in out front." —Captains Myers and McDonald had truly performed the big bluff of the campaign.

All during the course of these dispatches, Federal Col. George Gordon, one of Jackson's West Point classmates, pressed Banks to retreat, but Banks kept replying, "I must develop the force of the enemy." Gordon later remembered that "no argument could suppress this monotonous utterance." Not until the morning of the

24th did Banks acknowledge the danger and grandiloquently declare he was entering "the lists with the enemy in a race for the possession of Winchester"—still, his hesitation at Strasburg was not without unintentional benefit.

After all, where was Jackson? Why was Banks not bagged at Strasburg? Stonewall was following orders. From the beginning, his instructions had been to prevent Banks from leaving the Valley. If Jackson drove headlong to cut Banks off from Winchester, the Federals might have simply marched due east through Front Royal and out of the Valley. That Banks would try to slip through in such a way should have seemed improbable, yet Jackson had to wonder what other reason was keeping him in Strasburg. Even Jackson failed to realize that his own feints and secrecy had, for the moment, pinned Banks in place.

Yet, despite orders and Banks lethargy, Jackson still knew the logical route of escape for Banks was straight down the Valley Turnpike to Winchester, and he sent cavalry scouting accordingly. He also sent Ewell on the direct, diagonal route from Front Royal to Winchester, with orders to remain within supporting distance of Jackson's own division near Front Royal. Word was not long in coming. At 11 a.m. on the 24th, the Confederte patrols reported large Federal formations passing through Newtown on the Valley Turnpike in full retreat northward.

All became instantly clear, and Jackson immediately determined to cut the Federal column at Middletown. He sent Ashby's cavalry, Chew's horse artillery, part of the Rockbridge Artillery and the Louisiana Tigers to do the job. But when they struck at about 3 p.m., they struck only the rear elements of Banks' retreating army. Not at first realizing this, Jackson came up and directed his men to press the Federals back toward Strasburg, but what they were pressing turned out to be the rear portion of Banks' rear guard.

The pursuit north failed to come off. Ashby's ill-disciplined troopers were busy looting, as were Jackson's exhausted, poorly equipped, poorly fed infantrymen. Taylor said, "The gentle 'Tigers' were looting right merrily diving in and out of wagons with the activity of rabbits in a warren — an occupation abandoned on my approach — and, in a moment, they were in line, looking as solemn and virtuous as deacons at a funeral."

At this point, the flawed command structure of the Valley Army was becoming obvious by confusion. Jackson was still commanding his own division, and in battle, such a command was demanding and detracted from his command of the army. So, at 4:30 p.m. he ordered Ewell not to "advance any nearer Winchester . . . There seems to be still a considerable body of the enemy advancing on us from Strasburg." Then, at 5:45 p.m: "Major-General Jackson requests that you [Ewell] will at once move with all your force on Winchester." And, finally, "near Sunset," he sent Ewell word to "come on as you propose, by the Newtown road. Our [Jackson's Division] infantry is up."

It was too late; Banks had escaped. Never again would Jackson underestimate the impact of his own plans or overestimate the intentions of his enemies. Banks had escaped to fight another day, but Jackson would see that it would be the next day, Sunday, 25 May 1862.

Banks made his stand in the hills just south of Winchester, apparently to protect his army's stores—there was no other plausible reason, unless, of course, he was valuing real estate more than men, just as Fremont had in the mountains. Despite Banks' erroneous belief that Ewell and Jackson were on separate sides of Massanutten, he knew they would be united in front of Winchester and outnumber him by more than two to one, approximately 16,000 to 7,000. He knew that no sizable Federal force was within supporting distance, and he had not had time to fortify as at Strasburg. Still, he behaved as though his army was in strong defenses on friendly soil, and he apparently never even considered a voluntary retreat.

Although Jackson had been perplexed by Banks' hesitation at Strasburg, he was aided by Banks' stand at Winchester. But unaware of Banks' "assistance," Jackson pushed his men hard during the night of the 24th and the early hours of the 25th, saying, "I am obliged to sweat them tonight, that I may save their blood tomorrow." He was concerned as much about Banks entrenching as he was about Banks escaping.

The First Battle of Winchester (two more battles would be fought there later in the war) was never a near thing; neither was it a tactical masterpiece. Most of Jackson's Division plus Taylor's brigade deployed west of the Valley Turnpike, while Ewell's division, a mile to the east, proceeded forward on its own, under Jackson's broad directive to "attack at daylight."

Jackson, primarily playing the role of division commander, sent two of his own brigades and artillery forward to occupy a hill southwest of the city, but they came under intense fire from Federals on the next set of hills to the north. At this point, Jackson went for his "third division," Taylor's brigade, which was already advancing toward the "sound of the guns." He pointed to the enemy dominated height, saying only, "You must carry it." Taylor marched his men to the west, behind the Confederate-held hill, and around to the right flank of the Federals. There, at the base of the Federals' hill, the Louisianans formed up and Taylor ordered, "Attention, forward march." Federal cavalry struck his left; two companies of the 8th Louisiana stopped them. Undaunted, and with Pelican banners waving, the balance of the brigade steadily and inexorably drove on. They had not even let loose a volley when Taylor's next command came: "Forward, double quick, charge!" Private John Worsham observed from the Confederate-held hill: "That charge of Taylor's was the grandest I saw during the war." It was also effective. The Federals withdrew, and Jackson ordered a general advance of the entire Confederate line: "Let's hollar. Order forward the whole Army to the Potomac!"

Over on the right flank, Ewell's men had started forward in the morning as ordered, but the going was slow due to a dense fog along Abraham's Creek. By the time of Taylor's charge, however, the fog was finally lifting, and Ewell's men were breaking the Federal left, a fact which undoubtedly influenced the Federal actions in Taylor's sector.

Defeated on both flanks and facing a general assault up and down the line, the Federals broke and streamed down the reverse slopes of their hill defenses into Winchester — Confederates close behind. The citizens of Winchester were so happy, Worsham said, "it seemed that joy had overcome fear" as they poured into the bullet-showered streets to welcome their Southern sons — literally in many cases when the Stonewall Brigade's 5th Virginia Regiment, filled with Winchester soldiers, charged down the streets. Incredibly, it was preceded by its famous musicians, the Stonewall Brigade Band.

Taylor wrote of his own troops' entrance: "A buxom, comely dame, of some five-and-thirty summers, with bright eyes and tight ankles, and conscious of these advantages, was especially demonstrative, exclaiming, 'Oh! you are too late — too late!' whereupon a tall creole from the Teche sprang from the ranks of the Eighth Louisiana, just passing, clasped her in his arms, and imprinted a sounding kiss on her ripe lips, with 'Madame, je n'arrive jamais trop tard (Madam, I never arrive too late)!'"

Banks' army was routed, and Jackson looked for Ashby: "Never was there such a chance for cavalry. Oh, that my cavalry was in place." But his cavalry was not in place. Ashby was off chasing Federal cavalry, and Ewell's cavalry under Brig. Gen. George Steuart was idly lounging. Jackson sent Sandie Pendleton with orders for Steuart to "ride," but Steuart refused, stating his immediate commander, Ewell, must issue the orders. He could hardly be faulted, considering Ewell's earlier, all-too-vocal doubts about Jackson's sanity. Apparently, Ewell's opinion had changed during the conferences before the march to Front Royal, but he had not had time to apprise his subordinates of his reassessment. Still Ewell was furious when informed of Steuart's behavior.

Eventually, Ashby returned and Steuart received Ewell's orders, but the pursuit began too late. The intervening time had been sufficient for Banks to reform his army north of Winchester for an orderly retreat to the Maryland side of the Potomac. Even so, Jackson had bagged a third of Banks' army, and the remnants would not fight again in the Valley Campaign.

THE COST

Confederate: 68 killed, 329 wounded, 3 missing — total 400 (including the Battle of Front Royal and skirmishes 23 - 25 May 1862)..

Federal: 46 killed, 195 wounded, 1,025 missing — total 1,227 (see note, Chapter IX. The Battle of Front Royal).

Once again Jackson the strategist had prevailed, and once again Jackson the tactician, hampered by an unwieldy command structure, had delegated much of the battle's conduct — intentionally with Ewell and unintentionally with Ashby.

His McDowell operations had compelled the Federal forces in Northern Virginia to stretch, but at Front Royal and Winchester, he effectively punctured the encroaching Federal arc, thereby dividing the armies of Gen. Fremont and Gen. McDowell. Clearly, they would have to plug the gap left **by Banks' defeat — or so it seemed.**

XI. STRASBURG: MR. LINCOLN'S TRAP

"The army under your command encourages us to hope for all which men can achieve."
— **Jefferson Davis to Stonewall Jackson**

From Mississippi to Virginia, a blanket of blue formed a smothering arc that spring of 1862. The major Confederate armies were all on the defensive, and hopes were waning.

In Richmond, Gen. Johnston, now reinforced to 60,000 men, was facing McClellan's 100,000 Federals just outside Richmond while 40,000 more (including Shields' division, now totalling 10,000 men) under McDowell were marching south from Fredericksburg. Accordingly, Johnston was planning a battle of desperation for 29 May. Regardless of odds, he was compelled to strike before McDowell joined McClellan, although not even he expected success. The Confederate government was poised for evacuation, the citizens of Richmond were preparing for surrender, and only one man, far away in the Shenandoah Valley, was in a position to save the Southern Nation.

Stonewall Jackson had cracked the Federal arc at its weakest point, a weakness which he had caused. The breakthrough at Front Royal spelled doom for Banks, isolation for Fremont and a threat to McDowell's supply line with Washington. He could not be ignored, and the acting Federal general-in-chief, Abraham Lincoln, turned temporarily from Richmond and decided to remove the Jackson thorn once and for all. So even before Banks' disaster at Winchester, Lincoln was decided:

"May 24, 1862 — 5 p.m.
Major-General McDowell, Fredericksburg:

General Fremont has been ordered by telegraph to move from Franklin on Harrisonburg to relieve General Banks, and capture and destroy Jackson's and Ewell's forces.

You are instructed, laying aside for the present the movement on Richmond, to put 20,000 men in motion at once for the Shenandoah.... Your object will be to capture the forces of Jackson and Ewell.... The information thus far received here makes it probable that if the enemy operate actively against General Banks you will not be able to count upon much assistance from him....

A. LINCOLN."

McDowell acknowledged the order at 6 p.m. and followed-up with a dispatch 3½ hours later that stated in part: "I am entirely beyond helping distance of General Banks. . . . It will take a week or ten days... to get to the valley. . . , and by that time the enemy will have retired. I shall gain nothing for you there, and shall lose much for you here."

McDowell's plea was in vain, however, because Jackson and his little army had done the impossible, and the counterrotation of the Federal armies back toward the Shenandoah was about to commence. Lincoln was paying for his earlier errors of stripping Shields from Banks and of sending Blenker's Division to Fremont rather than Banks. Jackson's McDowell operations had caused these actions, but Lincoln was finally beginning to understand this, and he was correct in realizing Jackson had to be dealt with. As Lincoln said, Jackson had punched a "gap" in the Federal lines at Front Royal.

Jackson was in a position to defeat Fremont and Banks separately or to threaten the nearly undefended city of Baltimore or the weakly defended city of Washington. And if McDowell continued toward Richmond, the farther he would go, the more vulnerable his supply line would be to attack from Jackson.

Certainly, it was quite reasonable to expect the Confederates to exploit their successes in one or more of these ways. In fact, on 25 May, Secretary of War Stanton twice sent queries to McDowell: "Is it not probable Anderson's force (the small Confederate screening unit south of Fredericksburg) has left your front and gone by railroad and thence up to Culpeper and across to join Jackson and Ewell, instead of going south?"

Positive confirmation of this seemed to be contained in Federal Brig. Gen. John Geary's continual dispatches. Geary, who commanded a small brigade-sized force of all arms just east of the Blue Ridge at White Plains, cabled Stanton on the 26th: "...Jackson advancing with a large force through Middleburg to cut off my communication by Aldie Gap and Hopewell Gap (in the Bull Run Mountains). This force is estimated at at least 20,000...." He continued 20 minutes later with: "...There are also heavy forces south of me, and I cannot hope successfully to resist the combined elements against me. I might make Manassas...."

If Geary was correct, then Jackson was moving east and Anderson was reinforcing him from the south. Lincoln believed him and advised McDowell the same day: "Dispatches from Geary just received have been sent you. Should not the remainder of your forces, except sufficient to hold the point at Fredericksburg, move this way — to Manassas Junction or Alexandria?" — On the 24th, Lincoln had only ordered two of McDowell's four divisions into the Shenandoah.

But McDowell had assembled an accurate assessment and so notified Lincoln. He noted that Anderson's Confederates had gone to "Richmond! Richmond! Richmond! to take part in the big battle that is about to come off." And, he continued, "The forces in the upper part (meaning the north, which was actually the lower part) of the valley are those under Jackson, Ewell, and perhaps Ed. Johnson. Major-General Shields, who has had to do with them, estimates them at 16,000."

His assessment was correct, but it went unheeded — and perhaps, properly so. Regardless of the Valley Army's size, Jackson's tenet was holding true: "...repeated victory will make it invincible," or at least make it seem so, and it certainly seemed so after Winchester.

But Jackson and his "foot cavalry" knew when to go slowly. He had acted, and it was time to await his enemy's reactions. He had reduced their options, for neither Banks' defeated remnant across the Potomac at Williamsport, nor a hastily assembled conglomeration at Harper's Ferry under Brig. Gen. Saxton were militarily viable; Fremont was showing little inclination to act since the Battle of McDowell, and Blenker's division was behaving poorly; so it remained to see what Lincoln would do with Gen. McDowell. If Jackson's operations brought McDowell to the Valley, then Jackson would have accomplished all that Jefferson Davis, Robert E. Lee and Joe Johnston had desired. If not, if McDowell proceeded "on to Richmond," Jackson's eyes and army would most certainly have turned eastward, toward Washington.

About this time, he received a congratulatory dispatch from Johnston that included: "If you can threaten Baltimore and Washington, do so . . . McClellan is near and McDowell reported advancing from Fredericksburg." However, McDowell was marching for the Valley, not Richmond, and he was doing so with three divisions, not two. His fourth division had made a southward demonstration and returned to Fredericksburg, and it was this movement Johnston was addressing. (This dispatch also contained an interesting footnote: "Time will be gained and saved by addressing me always instead of the government").

Geary's fears had prevailed with Lincoln, and they continued to prevail, until even McDowell was affected. When, on 30 May, McDowell sent orders to bring a third division, Brig. Gen. Rufus King's, to the Valley, he included: "Jackson, Ewell, and Johnson are near Winchester with 30,000 men." He had at last accepted Geary's erroneous figures.

Meanwhile, Jackson had ignored an old gentleman's warnings on the 27th about McDowell's change of direction and on the following day he pressed on to Harper's Ferry, driving Saxton's men back on the heights south of the town. Still, messengers kept arriving with confirmation of McDowell's approach. Apparently, Jackson was intent upon hanging on until the last moment. He was the bait luring McDowell, and he played his part fully, lest his pursuer lose interest.

Leaving the Stonewall Brigade to demonstrate in front of Harper's Ferry, Jackson finally ordered the Valley Army south on the 30th. Simultaneously, he dispatched his friend and volunteer aide, Confederate Congressman Alexander Boteler, to Richmond with a plea for reinforcements sufficient to "transfer this campaign from the banks of the Potomac to those of the Susquehanna." He had performed his mission well, and by the time Richmond could react with meager assistance, there would be more than 60,000 Federals in or near the Shenandoah.

For McDowell, it was a period of conflicting objectives. Lincoln had wired him on the 28th: "...for you it is a question of legs. Put in all the speed you can." But speed of movement and concentration of forces were incompatible, especially since Ord's division had been routed through Alexandria — a situation partly due to Lincoln's wishes and partly to McDowell's choice. In any event, McDowell's lead division of 10,000 men under Brig. Gen. Shields could hardly close the trap alone against what were believed to be 30,000 Confederates. Nonetheless, Shields proceeded to Front Royal.

There, Jackson had posted the 12th Georgia, the regiment that had suffered so terribly at the Battle of McDowell. They were poorly served by their colonel at Front Royal. When Shields' division struck on the 30th, he retreated without a fight, though he knew time and distance were critical to the Valley Army. As a result, a number of his men were captured, a few of the Federals captured at the Battle of Front Royal were freed and Belle Boyd was taken prisoner. So when the colonel reported in, Jackson had good reason for placing him under arrest.

Still, Shields alone could not be a threat, and neither could Fremont, as both he and they knew. And where was Fremont? He was not at Harrisonburg where Lincoln had ordered him. Fremont, in his isolated position, had faced a dilemma. If he went to Harrisonburg, his army would be alone in the Valley to face Jackson. Fremont knew that his troops were certainly not up to that on an equal basis let alone if Jackson, in fact, had 30,000 men. Next, he could not cross into the Valley between Harrisonburg and Strasburg because, as noted, Jackson's map maker, Hotchkiss, had blockaded the passes during the McDowell operations. And finally, Lincoln's orders did say to come to Banks aid, so Fremont took the direct route via Moorefield.

Lincoln, of course, was furious. On the 27th, he wired: "I see you are at Moorefield. You were expressly ordered to march to Harrisonburg. What does this mean?"

Fremont shot back: "My troops were not in condition to execute your order otherwise than has been done.... The men had had so little to eat that many were weak.... Having for the main object, as stated in your telegram, the relief of General Banks, the line of march followed was a necessity...."

He followed this up the following day, explaining that subsequent to Lincoln's orders, Banks had retreated from Winchester. Also, he noted, of "the different roads to Harrisonburg all but one, and that one leading southward, had been obstructed by the enemy...." And, he said, "My troops were utterly out of provisions."

On the 29th, Fremont reported "stragglers, hundreds of whom from Blenker's division strewed the roads," had depleted his ranks. Jackson had indeed little to fear from Fremont.

In Washington, Lincoln saw his trap unravelling, yet he had no choice but to acquiesce in Fremont's move on Strasburg. Then, on the 30th, word came from Saxton at Harper's Ferry that "the rebels are in line of battle in front of our lines." There was still time to trap Jackson, and Lincoln forwarded Saxton's report to both Fremont and McDowell with identical addenda: "It seems the game is before you."

Once again Lincoln was wrong. The "game" was already shifting back to Richmond. With the threat of McDowell's army gone, Gen. Johnston was able to revise his plan for dealing with McClellan. Instead of throwing everything at the mass of McClellan's forces in desperation, he was able to concentrate against one isolated part of them at the Battle of Seven Pines on 31 May, the same day Shields entered Front Royal. However, Johnston's plan, although initially successful, went awry, and he was seriously wounded. On that day, fate flew on a bullet — Johnston was replaced by Gen. Robert E. Lee. At last Jackson would have only one commander. (Johnston would go on to fight Maj. Gen. Sherman in one of the great defensive campaigns of the war).

Back in the Valley, Ashby was performing yeoman service. He drove in Shields' pickets northwest of Front Royal and lured one Federal brigade toward Winchester, and this helped forestall Shields' move on Strasburg. Further, Shields, believing he was outnumbered by Jackson, was waiting for Ord's division to come up.

The other half of the trap, Fremont's army, was having an equally difficult time closing on its prey. These troops were trudging over the Shenandoah Mountains in a terrible storm, and this hardly improved their already difficult supply and morale problems.

This Federal lethargy was becoming clear to Jackson. His successes had cowed them, but he was not to be lulled, and he did not let up on his men. Jackson's foot cavalry continued to speed south, up the macadamized Valley Turnpike, and Jackson looked ahead to the next threat. Shields, with McDowell's other divisions in support, could push up the Luray Valley and cut the Valley Army off from Richmond. This possibility allowed little margin for Southern error, but error entered just the same. It did so in the person of Jedediah Hotchkiss.

Jackson had sent his cartographer to retrieve the Stonewall Brigade from Harper's Ferry, but the mapmaker — the army's guide — became lost, and the most critical commodity of the moment — time — was squandered (This and more is the "fog of war"). Now the Stonewall Brigade was coming on hard to catch up. The road had to be kept open for them. Fremont had to be kept out of Strasburg. The task fell to Ewell, who was anxious for the opportunity, however, he was unconditionally ordered to avoid becoming heavily engaged. It was a time for escaping.

On the morning of 1 June, Ewell's division swung westward from Strasburg to face Fremont, this though his command was far from full strength after hard, "Jackson marching." One of his cavalry officers, Col. Thomas Munford (who would later replace Ashby), wrote: "Hundreds of our best infantry fell by the wayside, but (overcoming their instinctive feud with the infantry, the riders) would help them, often taking them up behind them on their horses, or carrying their rifles or allowing them to hold on and be supported by the stirrups as they limped forward."

Yet despite such depletion, Ewell bested Fremont. Gen. Taylor called it a "walkover," and later wrote: "The prisoners taken in our 'promenade' were Germans — speaking no English — . . . In the Federal army was a German corps — the Eleventh [which Blenker's division would join] — . . . and this corps was, on both sides, called 'The Flying Dutchmen.' Since the time of Arminius, the Germans have been a brave people . . . but they require a cause and leaders." Blenker's division had proven to be even more ineffective than expected, and Germans in the Valley Army delighted in this, just as Marylanders against Marylanders had at Front Royal, and Irishmen against Irishmen would at Port Republic. There was more than one civil war going on in the Shenandoah Valley that year.

Fremont was pushed back, and Shields failed to push forward. So Strasburg was held while the men of the Stonewall Brigade, stretching the limits of human endurance, kept coming — the 2nd Virginia Regiment marched 35 miles in 18 hours, and it did so without rations.

On 1 June, as Ewell was going into action, the "lost brigade" was approaching Middletown when a rider suddenly appeared on the road ahead. The Stonewall Brigade's exhausted stalwarts could only assume the worst: Federal cavalry had caught them. But then a voice bellowed, "Is that General Winder coming up?" It was a known voice. It was Ashby's voice, and relieved, thankful, affirmatives were shouted in reply. And Ashby, sharing the sentiment, exclaimed, "Thank God for that!"

Lincoln's trap was a colossal failure. The forces of Banks and Saxton did not join in after reporting to Lincoln that their troops were not up to it. Neither was Fremont's command ready to face Jackson, but he failed to say so. All of the commanders, from Lincoln on down, feared battle with Jackson on an equal footing, yet he ordered Fremont's 15,000 men and Shields' 10,000 into Jackson's path — and this when the Valley Army was believed to be 30,000 strong. Lincoln's intelligence gathering and assessing was, flawed, his plan was unrealistic and his command and coordination was amateurish.

McDowell had been right, and by 1 June there were more than 60,000 Federals in or on the way to the Shenandoah Valley just to contend with Jackson's 16,000. Then again, had McDowell's men not gone there, where might Jackson have gone?

XII. BETWEEN TWO ARMIES: THE BATTLES OF CROSS KEYS AND PORT REPUBLIC

"... We must aid a gallant man if we perish."
— Gen. Robert E. Lee, referring to Maj. Gen. Stonewall Jackson

Jackson's retreat south, up the Valley, was not a run; neither was it a stroll. Rain was pouring down, and Fremont, displaying his best performance of the campaign, began nipping at Jackson's heels. However, Jackson's signal detachment atop Massanutten Mountain confirmed that Shields' men were strung out and struggling on mud roads in Luray Valley. Meanwhile, the Confederates were on the macadamized turnpike. So Fremont aside, the question was not how to beat Shields to Port Republic, but how best to deal with Shields once arriving there.

Jackson began looking ahead to the next stage of the campaign even as he was running the gauntlet at Strasburg. He saw the importance of Massanutten Mountain and the Forks of the Shenandoah, and he saw the importance of the south Fork bridges.

It was about this point that the campaign began to resemble one operation of Napoleon's Italian Campaign. In that operation, two Austrian armies, separated by mountains and a large lake, descended upon Napoleon, who then proceeded to defeat each of them separately. The potential analogy could not have been lost on Jackson, the professor of military history.

With Shields' division — followed far behind by two more of McDowell's divisions — marching up the east side of Massanutten Mountain, and with Fremont marching up the west side, the Napoleonic analogy was irresistible, and only interdiction was required to duplicate the situation. To keep his enemies separated, it was necessary to block the roads and burn the bridges between the two Federal forces. And Ashby, now promoted to brigadier general, had proven to be very adept at this. Even so, Jackson sent Col. Crutchfield, his chief of artillery, to confirm Ashby's work. Jackson had previously lamented that Ashby had "such bad discipline and attaches so little importance to drill that I regard it as a calamity to see him promoted."

Then, as Richmond suspected and perhaps Jackson hoped, Ashby rose to the occasion, and for the few remaining days of his life, performed the best work of his career. So, with Crutchfield along, Ashby burned the White House and Columbia bridges that spanned the South Fork between Luray and New Market.

Next, Jackson reported, "On June 2 the enemy's (Fremont's) advance came within artillery-range and commenced shelling our rear guard, which caused most of the cavalry (under Steuart) and that part of the artillery nearest the enemy to retreat in disorder. This led General Ashby to one of those acts of personal heroism and prompt resource which strikingly marked his character. Dismounting from his horse, he collected from the road a small body of infantry from those who from fatigue were straggling behind their commands." With these 50 exhausted men, Ashby stopped the Federal pursuit for the day, and Jackson, having transferred the Second and Sixth Virginia Cavalry (from Steuart of Ewell's division) to Ashby, placed him "in command of the rear guard."

On 3 June, Ashby blew the bridge over the North Fork near New Market to slow Fremont, but the Federals had a pontoon bridge in place the following morning. Fremont's cavalry crossed, but it was 4 June and the fourth day of rain and the pontoons soon washed out. Even so, Jackson left the stranded Federal cavalry alone and, instead, turned his attention back to Shields, sending some of Ashby's troopers to burn the South Fork bridge at Conrad's Store. The Second Italian Campaign analogy was now complete.

On 5 June, Jackson marched the army through Harrisonburg and turned southeast toward Port Republic, intentionally placing his force between two larger Federal forces. Fremont's pursuit continued unabated, and on the 6th, the Federal advance met the Confederate rearguard south of Harrisonburg. Both sides quickly called up infantry support. In the ensuing skirmish, the Federals were turned back, but the "Black Knight of Fauquier," Brig. Gen. Turner Ashby fell. His horse had been killed, so Ashby, the cavalier, died at the head of an infantry regiment.

The fight near Harrisonburg stopped Fremont's effective pursuit, perhaps to Jackson's chagrin, for he spent the following day unsuccessfully trying to lure Fremont into a general engagement.

As Sunday, 8 June dawned, Jackson, in the words of Sandie Pendleton, was "completely broken down" from exhaustion as a result of the long, harrowing, wet retreat up the Valley. And exhaustion was flawing his judgment.

Port Republic sits between the North River and South River at the point where they join and become the South Fork of the Shenandoah River. As such, the bridge there was crucial to Jackson. Still, he kept his army northwest of the North River, placing only a few pickets and a few cavalry patrols — and incredibly, himself, his staff and the army's wagon trains — south of the river in and around Port Republic. That morning, Jackson and his thin veil of soldiers were surprised when Shields' cavalry stormed into the town.

This was the great "almost" of the campaign. Jackson was nearly captured as the Federals gained possession of the Port Republic side of the North River Bridge. These Federals were aggressive, but poorly led, and they failed to even attempt the destruction of the bridge (Col. S.S. Carroll, the commander of Shields' advance brigade, claimed he had been ordered to leave the bridge intact so Shields and Fremont could unite). They brought their artillery up to it, but by then Jackson had guns in place on the bluffs across from them. At this point, Jackson yelled to the Federal gunners: "Bring that gun up here. Bring that gun up here, I say." Some men later claimed he was yelling at his own gunners; some say he thought the Federals were Confederates; and some say he was simply trying to bluff the enemy. Regardless of his intent, the Federals did not comply, and instead elevated their guns and fired. Stonewall's next command was unquestionably to his own men: "Let 'em have it!"

Next, his infantry came up, and he calmly commanded, "Charge right through, Colonel." He was, at least temporarily, himself again, even if only due to the surge of excitement.

Meanwhile, the Battle of Cross Keys had commenced. Ewell's division was posted at Cross Keys, just northwest of Port Republic, when Fremont struck. Ewell had around 5,000 men, which Jackson reinforced to around 6,000, but against him, Fremont had available between 12,000 and 15,000 men. Even though Fremont did not attack until he heard Carroll's guns, he claimed he was facing "Jackson's entire force," and the Federal tactics reflected this. Gen. Taylor called Fremont's attack "feeble in the extreme." Fremont committed only five of 24 regiments he had on hand, and these five were all from Blenker's division. They ran on the second volley.

THE COST

Confederate: 41 killed, 232 wounded, 15 missing — total 288.
Federal: 114 killed, 443 wounded, 127 missing — total 684.

A reinvigorated Jackson had Napoleonic plans for the 9th. He would leave a covering force at Cross Keys, strike Shields, then recross the river and finish off Fremont. Fremont cooperated; **Shields' men did not.**

Two brigades were sufficient to cow Fremont, while the rest of the Valley Army marched into Port Republic, then across a makeshift bridge over the South River to engage Shields. Only Shields' two most advanced brigades, approximately 3,000 men under Col. Carroll and Brig. Gen. Erastus B. Tyler, with the latter commanding, were present. As at Kernstown, they were ready. As at Kernstown, Jackson committed his men without first reconnoitering, and, as at Kernstown, he paid dearly for the error.

Brig. Gen. Winder's Stonewall Brigade went in, confident of a quick kill, when artillery opened up on its right flank and raked its lines. Seven Federal guns had been concealed on a coaling (a wood-burning site) part way up a ridge. Winder tried to dislodge them, but the guns were supported by infantry, and he failed. The Stonewall Brigade was being decimated. The Rockbridge Artillery weathered the rain of metal with the brigade, and one of the gunners even made light of it: "Ned, that isn't making batter-cakes is it?" This intrepid jester was Pvt. (later Capt.) Robert E. Lee, Jr.

Jackson acknowledged the changed situation and changed his plans. There would be no time for Fremont that day, and he ordered all of the Valley Army south of the North River and South Fork, with the North River Bridge to be burned behind them. Brig. Gen. Taylor's men were already coming at the run, and when they arrived, Jackson sent one regiment to bolster Winder. As for the rest, Jackson said to Jed Hotchkiss, "Take General Taylor around and take those batteries."

About then, Winder ordered a preemptive charge, but was soon stopped and the brigade started disintegrating to the rear. This was only halted by Ewell's timely arrival with more reinforcements. The Federal counterattack was stopped, then it turned on Ewell, and his men were forced into the woods below the coaling. At last the Stonewall Brigade's 33rd Regiment, which had lost its way, finally came up and bolstered the brigade.

By then Taylor had taken the coaling, lost the coaling, taken the coaling, lost it and finally retaken it. Then, the victorious Federals on the plain below turned their attention to him and prepared to charge. Taylor described it: "Wheeling to their right, with colors advanced, like a solid wall they marched straight upon us. There seemed nothing left but to set our backs to the mountain and die hard." But, "At the instant, crashing through the underwood, came Ewell, outriding staff and escort. He secured reenforcement (sic), and was welcomed with cheers... Loud Confederate shouts reached our delighted ears; and Jackson, freed from his toils, came like a whirlwind, the enemy in rapid retreat."

THE COST

Confederate: 93 killed, 693 wounded, 36 missing — total 822.
Federal: 67 killed, 393 wounded, 558 missing — total 1,018.

XIII. POSTERITY

". . . the record of Jackson's achievements in his Valley campaign has become a military classic in that it portrays the ideal leader in action."
— *The West Point Atlas of the Civil War*

The impossible was done. The rotation was reversed. Instead of moving east and southeast against Richmond and the Army of Northern Virginia, more than 60,000 Federal troops were in or on their way toward the Shenandoah Valley. And on 18 June 1862, it was Stonewall Jackson and the 15,000 men of the Valley Army who were on their way east — this in compliance with Gen. Lee's orders of 11 June: "The sooner you unite with this army the better." Jackson, the "bait" in the Valley, was about to become Jackson, the "hammer" on the Peninsula.

How Jackson accomplished what he did in the Valley can never be fully comprehended, but it can be described in a word: "diversion." On 15 June, Abraham Lincoln wrote Gen. Fremont:

"I think Jackson's game — his assigned work — now is to magnify the accounts of his numbers and reports of his movements, and thus by constant alarms keep three or four times as many of our troops away from Richmond as his own force amounts to. Thus he helps his friends at Richmond three or four times as much as if he were there. Our game is not to allow this." But it already had been allowed, and Lincoln's late assessment was by then nothing more than an obvious recitation of recent history.

In July Lincoln fired himself as general-in-chief, and later lamented to his secretary of war: "You and I, Mr. Stanton, have been trying to boss this job, and we have not succeeded very well with it."

Gen. McClellan seconded Lincoln's self assessment when testifying before a Congressional committee:

". . . had the command of General McDowell (40,000 men) joined the Army of the Potomac in the month of May by way of Hanover Courthouse from Fredericksburg, we would have had Richmond within a week after the junction" (and, theoretically, would have destroyed the Army of Northern Virginia). Of course, he did not say what mischief might have been expected from Jackson during that week. Unlike the course at West Point, the course of the war had lasted long enough for Jackson to pass up his classmate, McClellan.

The facts alone hardly tell the tale, but they are, nonetheless, exceedingly impressive: Beginning on 22 March 1862, the day before the Battle of Kernstown, and ending with the Valley Army's arrival on the Richmond front, 25 June, Jackson's army covered 676 miles in 48 marching days, fought six pitched battles, tied up more than 60,000 Federal troops and was the reason McClellan refused to unleash over 100,000 men against the Army of Northern Virginia, which was defending the Confederate capital. Stonewall Jackson and his never-more-than 17,000 men accomplished this unparalleled American feat despite receipt of too many orders, too few reinforcements and too little time and supplies.

At no time did the "fog of war" lift. Rather, the certainty of uncertainty prevailed, and Jackson reveled in it. For him, there was advantage in "fog." He was so secretive that even his friends had no idea what he was doing — and, in the case of the McDowell operations, what he had done.

Even so, Jackson sustained the worst breaks: Ashby was misinformed about enemy strength at Kernstown and in turn misinformed Jackson; underbrush kept Jackson's artillery out of the Battle of McDowell; the Confederate chain of command problems, in the form of conflicting orders to Ewell, nearly prevented the Front Royal operations; and at the Battle of Front Royal, an unreliable courier failed to bring up the artillery; propriety made Jackson's own chain of command unwieldy, and this affected his attempt to catch Banks north of Strasburg; Jackson's poorly equipped and poorly fed troops took to pillaging, rather than pursuing at critical times, especially during the pursuit of Banks to Winchester; a low-lying fog at the Battle of Winchester stalled Ewell's attack, and after that fight, Ashby's cavalry was out of position for the pursuit, and Steuart's cavalry refused to obey Jackson until Ewell confirmed the orders; then, while the Valley Army was trying to escape Lincoln's trap, his map maker, Hotchkiss, lost his way, and the Stonewall Brigade was nearly lost as a result; and the whole campaign concluded with Jackson's near capture at Port Republic, when his cavalry failed in its patrolling and screening duties.

Yet despite such "overestimations, underestimations, miscommunications and misunderstandings," Jackson fought friends and foes alike, and in the end, prevailed.

Of course, he was the recipient of some good luck: Flournoy's initiative at Front Royal; Federal Gen. Geary's fears and overestimations before Winchester; and there was the Federal failure to burn the bridge at Port Republic (but then, that might have accomplished nothing more than the destruction of Fremont's command, which would have been stranded on the opposite side to face Jackson alone). So good luck played a part, but in the realm and history of American warfare, never so small a part.

There were no tactical masterpieces in the Valley Campaign; those would come later (though not in the subsequent Peninsula Campaign). No, Jackson's Valley Campaign was a strategic masterpiece, the masterpiece of a military genius. It was a campaign that Claude Crozet, a Napoleonic veteran who had been a founder of VMI and an instructor at West Point, labeled as "extra-Napoleonic."

Jackson's genius seemed never to have been stretched, and each new situation seemed to call up solutions from untouched depths of his mind. His mind was a reservoir of retention, and as it grew at West Point, so it grew on the battlefield, and Gen. Taylor was correct in saying he "was ever superior to occasion.".

As Jackson absorbed, he created and became more than one genius. He displayed the wisdom of boldness at Kernstown; the forethought and multi-tiered thinking of a chess player in the moves from Swift Run Gap to McDowell; the finessing forte and political intrigue of a Talleyrand in his display of disobedience without insubordination just prior to the Front Royal operation; the Cromwellian singlemindedness and eye for the kill at Front Royal; the patient premeditation and cool calculation of a river-boat gambler in his role of the bait for Lincoln's trap at Strasburg; and the analytical and academic insight of a history professor when, at the end of the campaign, he duplicated part of Napoleon's Italian Campaign.

Finally, Stonewall Jackson's intentional self-entrapment and subsequent extrication at Cross Keys and Port Republic, ended his Valley Campaign — his masterpiece — with a virtual signature, and Richard Taylor could say, "What limit to set to his ability I know not" — and no one ever will.

ADDENDUM A. THE COMMANDERS

THE CONFEDERATES

Lt. Gen. Thomas Jonathan Jackson: Following the Valley Campaign (his earlier life is covered in the text), Jackson brought his men east to join Gen. Robert E. Lee's assault against McClellan's besieging Army of the Potomac. Known as the Seven Days battles, Lee repeatedly struck various exposed elements of McClellan's numerically superior army, but Jackson failed to display his usual promptness or aggresiveness. He had recently gone with very little sleep, and he was physically exhausted by his recent Valley operations, but, more significantly, he was a very independent general. He performed best when given general directives, rather than specific commands, and Lee thereafter **accommodated him**.

With McClellan stymied on the Peninsula, Lee sent Jackson north of Richmond to deal with Gen. Pope, the recently appointed commander of the Federal Army of Virginia which included the commands of McDowell, Banks and Fremont (although Fremont resigned rather than fight under Pope). Jackson engaged a portion of these forces at Cedar Mountain, then Lee brought up most of the balance of the Army of Northern Virginia in support and the Second Manassas Campaign began.

In perhaps the biggest gamble of the war, Lee split his forces, sending Jackson's corps on an extended flanking movement almost to the Shenandoah Valley, then back eastward through the Bull Run Mountains to Manassas Junction, between Pope's army and Washington. Jackson performed admirably. Placing his men in a railroad cut on a hill, he withstood Pope's massive onslaughts until Longstreet's corps came up in support.

The Federals were driven into the defenses of Washington, and Lee invaded Maryland. From Frederick, Maryland, Jackson was sent to capture the 12,000-man Federal garrison at Harper's Ferry, but, meanwhile, Lee's famous Lost Order fell into McClellan's hands. McClellan, who had returned from the Peninsula, absorbed Pope's army into the Army of the Potomac, and drove west against Lee's scattered forces. Jackson, having taken Harper's Ferry, rushed north to Sharpsburg where Lee was concentrating. There, near Antietam Creek, Jackson anchored the north flank and bore the brunt of the fighting. His fluid defense included counterattacks, ambushes and bluffs against overwhelming odds. Unquestionably, this was Jackson at his tactical best. McClellan was stopped, and the Army of Northern Virginia escaped.

December of this same year brought the Battle of Fredericksburg. Jackson commanded on the right where he established a defense in depth. So when his thin front line was attacked, he had ample troops available to counterattack. After he did so, the Federals to his front showed little inclination to renew the contest there, but foolishly flung themselves, instead, against Longstreet's all but impregnable positions on Marye's Heights. It was another Federal disaster, and it closed out a long year of fighting in the East.

1863 brought one major battle for Jackson: Chancellorsville. There, Lee and Jackson collaborated as never before. The Federals had crossed the Rappahannock west of the Confederate positions at Fredericksburg. Lee, drastically outnumbered, hurled what he could against them before they could emerge from the thick woods. With them momentarily stopped, Jackson was then sent with his men on a march in front of, alongside and behind the Federal positions. Once again Lee had split his outnumbered forces, and once again Jackson was his instrument. Stonewall and his men were confident though. They were going after those same troops they had come to disdain in the Valley, Blenker's men, now under Gen. O.O. Howard. And Jackson's confidence was well founded, because those Federals flew as they had before.

That evening, however, the South suffered what was perhaps its fatal blow. Lt. Gen. Thomas J. "Stonewall" Jackson, returning from a reconnaissance, was wounded by his own men. As he lay dying in the days that followed, Gen. Lee wrote, "He has lost his left arm; but I have lost my right arm" — and so too had the Confederacy. He died 10 May 1863. He could not be replaced.

Lt. Gen. Richard S. Ewell: He was born 8 February 1817 in Georgetown, D.C. and graduated from West Point in 1840. He fought in the Mexican War, the Indian Wars and the Civil War. He commanded a brigade at First Manassas and a division with Jackson in the Valley, the Seven Days and Second Manassas, where he lost a leg. Ewell was promoted and given the Second Corps upon Jackson's death in 1863. But this superb division commander was not suited for corps command, and he certainly was not Jackson, a fact Gen. Lee realized only too late. With Jackson, Lee's specific orders had evolved into general suggestions and broad directives, and Lee persisted in this manner with Ewell. But at Gettysburg, Ewell awaited specifics and hesitated to advance when Lee's orders to attack included the fatal proviso, "If possible." There was no mistaking Lee's meaning, however, when he said "Jackson was not there."

Ewell fought at the Wilderness and Spotsylvania, but thereafter commanded the Richmond defenses. He was captured at Sayler's Creek during the retreat to Appomattox. After the war, he retired to a farm near Spring Hill, Tennessee and died 25 January 1872.

Lt. Gen. Richard Taylor: Born 27 January 1826 near Louisville, Kentucky, he was the son of President Zachary Taylor. He graduated from Yale in 1845 and became his father's secretary during the Mexican War, after which he became a planter and state politician.

Taylor, a jovial, amiable individual, served under the taciturn Jackson in the Valley and the Seven Days. He was then sent to command the Department of West Louisiana. There, he gained his greatest fame when he defeated his and Jackson's old Valley opponent, Nathaniel P. Banks, in the Red River Campaign. As a result he was promoted and given command of the Department of Alabama and Mississippi, which he surrendered in May 1865.

Taylor's sister was Jefferson Davis' first wife. He died in New York 12 April 1879.

Brig. Gen. Turner Ashby: He was born 23 October 1828 in Fauquier County, Virginia. During the Civil War, his only major service was in the Shenandoah Valley. He was not a professional soldier, but he was a natural leader, a superb horseman and a man unsurpassed in personal bravery. Jackson wrote of him, "As a partisan officer I never knew his superior. His daring was proverbial, his power of endurance almost incredible, his tone of character heroic, and his sagacity almost intuitive in divining the purposes and movements of the enemy." And this came from the man who had opposed Ashby's promotion.

Ashby, the "Black Knight of Fauquier," did have his problems, and what Jackson did not say highlighted them. He did not drill or discipline his men, and as a result, they proved to be unreliable or absent during pitched battles. His most notable failure came at Winchester when he was not in position to follow up Jackson's victory.

On the other hand, he was an expert partisan. His intelligence gathering was usually accurate — with the notable exception just prior to the Battle of Kernstown — and his outpost and covering force duties were usually performed aggressively. His best performance came as the Valley Army escaped Lincoln's trap. Ashby, recently promoted brigadier general, drew Shields north as Jackson slipped away to the south, and later, he kept Fremont at bay. He was engaged in this activity when he was killed south of Harrisonburg, 6 June 1862.

THE FEDERALS

President Abraham Lincoln, General-in-Chief: He was the man who actually exercised field command, albeit from Washington, of the Federal forces in the Valley and was therefore Jackson's primary opponent during the campaign.

As a young Whig politician from Illinois, he proclaimed President Polk "talked like an insane man." He was referring to Polk's attempt to assert presidential authority over specific military actions during the Mexican War. Congress shared Lincoln's view, and Polk backed down, bringing presidential control of the military to its lowest point in American history.

Just 15 years later, as president, Lincoln proceeded to act almost without limit, reaching his peak of power 11 March 1862 when he replaced Maj. Gen. McClellan as general-in-chief with himself. But by July, the armies over which he exercised day to day control, the Federal armies in Virginia, had lost 10 battles.

Finally, on 23 July 1862, Lincoln replaced himself as general-in-chief with Maj. Gen. Henry Halleck. He later lamented to his secretary of war, "You and I, Mr. Stanton, have been trying to boss this job, and we have not succeeded very well with it." But then they had gone up against Robert E. Lee and Stonewall Jackson.

Lincoln was shot at Ford's Theater in Washington on 14 April 1865, and died the following day. An attempt was also made on the life of Secretary of State Seward. Some circumstantial evidence exists that points to Secretary of War Edwin Stanton as the ring leader of these assassination plots. Stanton directed the pursuit of Lincoln's assassin, John Wilkes Booth, and his accomplices, but the specifics of both the plot and pursuit are still unclear.

Maj. Gen. John C. Fremont: He was born 21 January 1813 in Savannah, Georgia to unmarried parents, a fact which would plague him politically for the rest of his life. He became an adventurer and explorer, the living embodiment of the concept of "manifest destiny." He married the daughter of Missouri's Senator Thomas Hart Benton. Benton, a man of like beliefs, financed his son-in-law's further western explorations, and Fremont became known as the Pathfinder of the West.

Prior to the outbreak of war with Mexico, Fremont, with apparently secret orders from President Polk, set out with a body of men to foment revolution in the Mexican Province of California. Displaying remarkable skill, Fremont did just that, but he refused to obey Brig. Gen. Stephen Kearny who arrived in California at the end of the campaign. He was courtmartialed and found guilty of mutiny. Although President Polk refused to testify for him — to have done so would have been an admission of war instigating — but he did pardon him.

Fremont soon became rich from gold found on his extensive California holdings, and he was elected to the U.S. Senate from the new state. He reached the apex of his new political career when, in 1856, he became the first, though unsuccessful, Republican presidential nominee.

When the Civil War came, his political strength more than his military background won him a major general's appointment from Lincoln. He was given command of the Department of the West with headquarters in St. Louis. Lincoln relieved him, however, when the Pathfinder issued an emancipation proclamation — Lincoln said the war was being waged to preserve the Union, not to free the slaves. Radical Republicans, however, forced Lincoln to appoint him to command of the Mountain Department. There, he was plagued by supply problems, Blenker's unreliable division and Lincoln's unrealistic expectations (see Chapter XI. Lincoln's Trap). Even so, Fremont could have done better, and his poor performance at Cross Keys was inexcusable.

After the Valley Campaign, he was placed under a man he despised, Maj. Gen. Pope, and he resigned. Following the war, he became the territorial governor of Arizona. He died in New York City 13 July 1890.

Maj. Gen. Nathaniel P. Banks: Born 30 January 1816 in Waltham, Massachusetts, he went to work as a bobbin boy in a textile factory. From this humble beginning, he worked his way up, becoming a U.S. Representative and later Speaker of the House, but he never shook the nickname, "Bobbin Boy." He was also one of the founders of the Republican Party, and by the Civil War, his political credentials and clout were surpassed only by Lincoln's.

In 1861, Lincoln was not elected by a majority, and the Republican hold on the North was at first only tenuous, and political allies were often won with the gift of high military rank. For this reason, and this reason alone, Lincoln appointed Banks, a man totally devoid of military training or experience, a major general, and entrusted the lives of Northern boys to his care. Confederate troops in the Valley soon took to contemptuously calling him Jackson's Commissary and Napoleon P. Banks.

Still, his poor performance in the Shenandoah was more a result of Lincoln's errors than his own. Perhaps realizing this, Lincoln later sent him to New Orleans to launch the ill fated Red River Campaign of 1864. This time his errors were his own, and he was soundly defeated by Maj. Gen. (later Lt. Gen.) Richard Taylor.

After the war he was returned to the House of Representatives by his faithful Massachusetts constituents, among whom he remained popular until his death 1 September 1894 in New York City.

Brig. Gen. James Shields: Born 10 May 1810 in Altimore, County Tyrone, Ireland, he rose to high political office in the United States, becoming a U.S. Senator from both Illinois and Minnesota. He was abrasive, explosive and firey, qualities which brought him to challenge Abraham Lincoln to a duel before the war (though it did not take place).

Unlike Banks, he was militarily experienced, having served in the Mexican War, but like Banks and Fremont, he owed his rank primarily to political influence. In Fremont, Banks and Shields, Lincoln courted constituencies in the West, the Northeast and the Midwest, respectively.

Shields was also quite boastful, and he made much of the Battle of Kernstown even though he had not been on the field. In fact, Shields never personally commanded troops in a pitched battle in the Valley. His subordinates won at Kernstown, and, because his troops were so strung out in the Luray Valley, they lost at Port Republic. As a result, Shields was soon relieved, and he resigned a year later. He became a U.S. Senator after the war and died in Oregon 1 June 1879.

ADDENDUM B:
JACKSON'S ORDERS OF BATTLE

THE BATTLE OF KERNSTOWN

Valley District: Maj. Gen. T.J. Jackson

Jackson's Division:
Maj. Gen. T.J. Jackson

Cavalry companies:
Col. Turner Ashby

1st (Stonewall) Brigade:
Brig. Gen. Richard B. Garnett

2nd Brigade:
Col. Jesse Burks

3rd Brigade:
Col. S.V. Fulkerson

THE BATTLE OF McDOWELL

Valley District: Maj. Gen. T.J. Jackson

Jackson's Division:
Maj. Gen. T.J. Jackson

1st (Stonewall) Brigade:
Brig, Gen. Charles S. Winder

2nd Brigade:
Col. John A. Campbell

3rd Brigade:
Brig. Gen. William B. Taliaferro

Army of the Northwest:
(treated as a division)
Brig. Gen. Edward Johnson

1st Brigade:
Col. Z.T. Conner

2nd Brigade:
Col. W.C. Scott

Valley Cavalry

THE BATTLES OF FRONT ROYAL, WINCHESTER, CROSS KEYS AND PORT REPUBLIC

Valley District: Maj. Gen. T.J. Jackson

Jackson's Division:
Maj. Gen. T.J. Jackson

1st (Stonewall) Brigade:
Brig. Gen. Charles S. Winder

2nd Brigade:
Col. John M. Patton (from 25 May)

3rd Brigade:
Brig. Gen. William B. Taliaferro

Third Division:
Maj. Gen. Richard S. Ewell

Elzey's Brigade:
Brig. Gen. Arnold Elzey

Scott's Brigade:
Col. W.C. Scott

Trimble's Brigade:
Brig. Gen. Isaac Trimble

Maryland Line:
Brig. Gen. George H. Stuart

Valley Cavalry:
Brig. Gen. Turner Ashby
(Brig. Gen. George H. Steuart
commanded Ewell's cavalry
24 May - 2 June, after which it
became part of Ashby's command)

Taylor's Brigade:
(part of Third Division,
but treated as
a separate division)
Brig. Gen. Richard Taylor

Department Artillery:
Lt. Col. Stapleton Crutchfield

ADDENDUM C: RANKS AND COMMANDS

CONFEDERATE	FEDERAL	COMMAND (AND SYMBOLS)	STRENGTH
Gen., Lt. Gen., Maj. Gen.	Maj. Gen.	XXXX ARMY	3,000 - 200,000
Lt. Gen., Maj. Gen.	Maj. Gen.	XXX Corps	5,000 - 25,000
Maj. Gen., Brig. Gen.		XX Division	2,500 - 12,000
Brig. Gen., Col.		X Brigade	1,000 - 5,000
Col., Lt. Col.		‖‖ Regiment	300 - 1,200
Lt. Col., Maj.		‖ Batallion	200 - 800
Capt., 1st Lt.		‖ Company	50 - 200

Akers, Frank and Scott, John, *The Battle of McDowell, May 8, 1862, A Terrain Study and Tour*. An unpublished manuscript. Property of the U.S. Army War College.

Boatner, Mark M., III, *The Civil War Dictionary*. David McKay Co., Inc., 1959.

Bowman, John S., ed., *The Civil War Almanac*, Gallery Books, 1983.

Boyd, Belle, *Belle Boyd in Camp and Prison*. Thomas Yoseloff, 1968.

Catton, Bruce, *The Civil War*. American Heritage Publishing Co., 1960.

Chambers, Lenoir, *Stonewall Jackson*. William Morrow & Co., 1959.

"Civil War." *American History Illustrated*. No date.

Clark, Champ, ed., *Decoying the Yanks, Jackson's Valley Campaign*. Time-Life Books, 1984.

Clauswitz, Karl von, *On War*. Random House, 1943.

Davis, Jefferson, *The Rise and Fall of the Confederate Government*. D. Appleton & Co., 1881.

Douglas, Henry Kyd, *I Rode with Stonewall*. Mockingbird Books, Inc., 1983.

Downer, Edward T., *Stonewall Jackson's Shenandoah Valley Campaign 1862*. Lee-Jackson Memorial Inc., 1974.

Eliot, Ellsworth, Jr., *West Point in the Confederacy*. G.A. Baker & Co.,Inc., 1941.

Esposito, Vincent J., ed., *The West Point Atlas of the Civil War*. Frederick A. Praeger, 1962.

Freeman, Douglas Southall, *Lee's Lieutentants—A Study in Command*. Charles Scribner's Sons, 1942-44.

Fuller, J.F.C., *Decisive Battles of the U.S.A.*. Harper & Brothers, 1942.

Henderson, G.F.R., *Stonewall Jackson and the American Civil War*. Longmans, Green, and Co., 1909.

Jomini, Henri, *The Art of War*. J.B. Lippencott Co., 1877.

Lee, Robert E., Clifford Dowdey, ed., *The Wartime Papers of R.E. Lee*. Bramhall House, 1961.

Long, E.B., *The Civil War Day by Day*. Doubleday & Co., Inc., 1971.

Robertson, James I., *The Stonewall Brigade*. Louisiana State University Press, 1963.

Robertson, James I., "Stonewall in the Shenandoah: The Valley Campaign of 1862." *Civil War Times Illustrated*, May 1972.

Schildt, John W., *Stonewall Jackson Day by Day*. Antietam Publications, 1980.

Tanner, Robert G., *Stonewall in the Valley*. Doubleday & Co., Inc., 1976.

Taylor, Richard, "Stonewall Jackson and the Valley Campaign." *N.A. Review*, Mar.-Apr. 1878.

United States War Department, *The War of the Rebellion: A Compilation of the Official Records of the Union and Confederate Armies*. The National Historical Society, 1971.

Warner, Ezra J., *Generals in Blue:Lives of the Union Commanders*. Louisiana State University Press, 1964.

Warner, Ezra J., *Generals in Gray: lives of the Confederate Commanders*. Louisiana State University Press, 1978.

Warren County Civil War Centennial Commemoration, *Battle of Front Royal*. Virginia Hale, 1962.

The Author

Capt. Douglas A. Cohn graduated from the United States Military Academy at West Point in 1968 and served in Vietnam 1969-1970. He was awarded two Silver Stars, the Vietnamese Cross of Gallantry and the Purple Heart, and he was retired due to disabling wounds. He tutored military history at West Point and he is now a nationally syndicated columnist and the editor of Associated Features. Capt. Cohn is the author of *15,000 Weeks: Looking Back in Northern Virginia.* He and his wife, Kathryn, have four children.